When The devil Whispers In Her Ear!

Janice S. Kieschnick

A family's journey through their daughter's battle with
anorexia and how, by the Grace of God, they overcome the
enemy and grow stronger in their faith.

*Cover Photo of Katelyn Kieschnick by her aunt
Sandra Kieschnick.*

Table of Contents

PREFACE 5

FORWARD 8

INTRODUCTION 11

1. THE VIEW FROM THE MOUNTAIN TOP 15

2. THE JOURNEY THROUGH THE VALLEY 19

3. MENDING THE BROKEN PIECES 27

4. THE POWER OF A MOTHER'S LOVE 34

5. ANOREXIA CANNOT TAKE OUR LOVE 45

6. FEAR NOT 53

7. THERE'S NO SUCH PLACE AS PERFECTVILLE ...61

8. HER TENDER HEART WAS BROKEN 68

9. FINDING THE SONG IN HER HEART 75

10. THE ROLLER COASTER RIDE 83

11. ANGEL OF HOPE 88

12. PART OF GOD'S PLAN 94

13. A SISTER'S LOVE 109

14. LANDEE'S STORY 114

15. FINDING LAUGHTER AMONG THE TEARS 118

16. CELEBRATION OF LIFE 122

17. THOU ANOINTEST MY HEAD WITH OIL 126

18. BITTERSWEET 131

19. FORGIVENESS 136

20. LEARNING TO DANCE IN THE RAIN 140

21. IN THE MIDST OF FIRE--GOD IS THERE 144

22. THE REASON FOR HOPE 149

EPILOGUE..156

Twelve Things People Don't Understand About An Eating
Disorder 160

VALUABLE TOOLS FOR FAMILIES..........................163

REFERENCES 167

"You planned evil against me, but God used those plans for my good..." Genesis 50:20 MSG

PREFACE

Has the devil ever whispered in your ear? Has he ever filled your mind with lies? The Bible tells us that Satan is a liar, the father of all lies, and he will deceive us in any way he can. So what does a Christian family do when Satan makes a personal visit into their home, with the intent to destroy them with his lies?

Four years ago, my family was devastated by a tragedy that would change our lives forever. Not a natural tragedy, not a man-made tragedy, but a super-natural tragedy brought into our lives by Satan, in the form of a disease known as anorexia. While trying to find the right treatment for our daughter, struggling to maintain our marriage, and protect our children from separation due to misinformation given to the Child Protective Services, I began to keep a journal as my only means of sanity.

Through these personal experiences, as documented in my journal, I have written this book, which focuses on the disease of anorexia, as manifested by Satan, and how God helped my family to fight this battle against the devil. You will notice that in the title, the word "devil" is not capitalized. This is because my book is not intended to glorify Satan, but everyone needs to know that he is very real, living on this earth, trying to destroy Christians, whether it is through our faith, our bodies or our minds.

I am not a well-known author. I am a mother who has

seen firsthand the terror in my daughter's eyes, and with the help of God, has helped to hush the voices in my daughter's head. My prayer is that this book will help other families dealing with tragedies in their lives and that all the glory will go to God for the miracles He has performed in our lives.

"I will praise you, O Lord, with all my heart; I will tell of all your wonders...My enemies turn back; they stumble and perish before you." Psalm 9: 1 & 3 NIV

DEDICATION

This book is dedicated to my husband, Trent, and our children, Tanner, Katelyn and Landee for never losing sight of God and for never losing faith during the most difficult year of our lives.

Sometimes we felt like we were being attacked by the enemy from all sides. Sometimes it felt like it was us against the world. Sometimes we wanted to give up and walk away, but we didn't. We fought together, we stayed together and we prayed together. Always remember, "A family that prays together, stays together!"

"A word spoken in encouragement is like apples of gold in settings of silver." Proverbs 25:11 NIV

ACKNOWLEDGEMENTS

A special "Thank You" to the people who helped us through this year:

Elizabeth Bay, R.D.L.D. Medical Nutrition Therapist-(Katelyn's Dietician)

Kim Macklin-(Family friend and survivor of anorexia and bulimia)

Reverend Paul Neuberger-(Pastor at St. Paul Lutheran Church)

Randall Schaffner, M.D.-(Family Doctor)

Linda Winfrey, M.A., L.P.C.-(Katelyn's counselor)

Friends and family who supported us and reached out to us through prayers, cards, phone calls, texts, emails, and hugs.

And to those who didn't--Never let your life get too busy that you miss the opportunity to reach out to someone who is hurting. Just a card, a phone call, a prayer, or a word of encouragement can make all the difference in someone's life!

"My ears had heard of you, but now my eyes have seen you." Job 42:5 NIV

FORWARD

Eating Disorders are illnesses that require identification and therapeutic tools for successful treatment and recovery. The earlier recognition and action increases the treatment outcomes. This story depicts the events and feelings of a family, and the caregivers in how an eating disorder effects the whole and are detrimental to all those involved. Recovery is possible and the ultimate goal for all victims of this illness. It is a process that requires on-going realization, support, and continued work towards a plan for maintaining healthy eating and functioning.

Treatment should be tailored to the individual needs of the person while consulting with clinically trained, educated and credentialed caregivers. The treatment approach selected, after much clinical research and consultation, was ideal for the personal situation of the individual and the family. People seeking treatment should identify the treatment approach that is successful for their needs. This book can assist others as they begin to understand and unfold the similarities of this disorder.

Lisa Puckett, M.Ed., LCDC

"Consider it pure joy whenever you face trials of many kinds, because you know that the testing of your faith develops perseverance." James 1:2-3 NIV

A MESSAGE FROM TRENT KIESCHNICK

As I was reading the following passage in the Bible, I immediately saw myself in this story. I was a father with a sick child, who didn't put my full trust and faith in Jesus. I didn't understand what that meant. I thought that somehow, I could handle the situation by myself.

"A man in the crowd answered, "Teacher, I brought you my son, who is possessed by a spirit that has robbed him of speech."

Jesus asked the boy's father, "How long has he been like this?"

"From childhood," he answered. "It has often thrown him into the fire or water to kill him. But if you can do anything, take pity on us and help us."

"If you can?" said Jesus. "Everything is possible for him who believes."

Immediately the boy's father exclaimed, "I do believe; help me overcome my disbelief!" Jesus rebuked the evil spirit and said, "I command you, come out of him and never enter him again."

The spirit shrieked, convulsed him violently and came out. The boy looked so much like a corpse that many said, "He's dead." But Jesus took him by the hand and lifted him to his feet, and he stood up.

After Jesus had gone indoors, his disciples asked him

privately, "Why couldn't we drive it out?" He replied, "This kind can come out only by prayer." Mark 9: 17, 21-29 NIV

When Katelyn first got sick, I didn't pray with a positive attitude knowing that Jesus would heal her. In fact, I don't think I even prayed at all. I remember that I did do a lot of worrying, whining, and complaining because I didn't understand the true meaning of turning everything over to God in prayer. I was raised to be a hard-worker and to get the job done right. Because I own a business, I was supposed to know how to fix everything and I had trained myself to be independent and not ask for help from anyone. I didn't understand that only God and prayer could heal my daughter.

I am grateful that God showed me, through this disease and through the faith of my seventeen year old daughter, that until we surrender our lives completely to God, we will never fully understand or experience God's power and grace.

"Be self-controlled and alert. Your enemy the devil prowls around like a roaring lion looking for someone to devour. Resist him, standing firm in the faith…" 1 Peter 5:8-9 NIV

INTRODUCTION

It's a hot, July night. Outside, the Texas heat is sweltering. Inside, the house is dark and quiet. Everyone is gone tonight. Trent is working late, Tanner is out with friends, and Landee is away at church camp. Lately, that's not so unusual. They all find places to go, places to hide, places to escape, but not me. Not that I don't want to escape. I fantasize about the motorcycle rider that I saw this afternoon while waiting at a stop light. I don't know him. I can't even see his face underneath his helmet, but as I glance at him in his leather gear, I imagine he is riding into the sunset, chasing an adventure. Just for a split second, I want to climb on the back of that motorcycle and ride with him. I want to be free from this nightmare. I want to escape. Of course, I don't. I can't. I know where I need to be. I know what I have to do. My daughter can't escape either, so we'll fight this battle together.

Katelyn is home now and she is exhausted. She has been at cheerleading practice all day and her deteriorating body aches. Her tiny frame can't take much more, so she goes to her room and collapses into bed.

Up until recently, it wasn't often that I had the house to myself. It's not often that the house is quiet and still. So, tonight, I sit alone in the silent, darkness and read another book about this devastating illness that has engulfed our lives. In the calm, I pretend that our lives are back to normal. I close my eyes and pretend that tomorrow everything will be alright, but I know in my heart this isn't true. I know in my heart, this is the calm before the storm. It's around ten o'clock now and the only light on is the reading lamp next to my chair. As I read, I desperately search for answers. Why is this happening to our family? Why is this happening to our daughter? I don't find the answers in the book that I'm reading tonight.

From Katelyn's room I hear a piercing scream, so piercing it startles me back into reality. I run to her room and turn on the light, half expecting to find a mouse. She is terrified of mice, but something more terrifying than that has gripped her mind. Tonight, the look I see on her face, the look I see in her eyes, tells me this is gut-wrenching fear. By now, Katelyn is sitting up in bed, she is crying and shaking and she tells me there was a man in her room. She describes him as extremely ugly, with a smirk-like grin on his face and he was lying on top of her, trying to smother her. With a trembling voice, she quivers, "He was real Mom! He was real! He was right here (as she pats her boney chest), he was right here, on top of me. I couldn't breathe! He was smothering me! He was ugly, with ugly teeth! He was real MOM!!!"

I sit beside her on the bed and wrap my arms around her. I rock her and comfort her, my beautiful seventeen year old daughter who is tormented by this disease. I brush the damp hair from her face. I tell her it will be okay because I'm here now, I love her, and I will take care of her. I think to myself, if only I knew for sure that everything would be okay. I tell her it was just a bad dream and I reassure her by checking under the bed and in the closet. I hold her and rock her until she drifts back to sleep, then I tiptoe out of her room, turn off the light and gently shut the door.

As I stand in the dark, quiet hall, tears stream down my face and I realize for the first time that evil is among us. I realize that the devil is present in my home and involved in this disease. It all makes sense now--the voices in Katelyn's head. The toxic words of self-loathe spewed from her mouth, but not in her voice. The agonizing, tear-filled hours spent apologizing for actions she can't control. Katelyn's vision tonight was NOT a dream- it was very real. The devil and his army of demons are trying to kill her by destroying her mind and her body.

Surprisingly, I'm not scared because what the devil doesn't know is that I'm prepared. I stand in that dark, quiet hall and I speak these words out loud, the same words that Jesus spoke many years ago when he was tempted by the devil in the desert, "Away from me, Satan!"

I say to the devil, out loud, "You WILL NOT stay in my home! You WILL NOT harm my children! You WILL NOT destroy my family...because we believe in someone more powerful than you, our Almighty God who WILL deliver us from this evil!!!"

And then, as if a guiding light has encircled me, I begin to realize that I have been looking for answers in the wrong books. The book we need is the Bible and who we need the most is God. He will help us to get through this. He will give us answers. He will comfort us, and most of all, He will heal our daughter … when the devil whispers in her ear!

13

"I have never met you, but I know your destructive powers.
I see your lies and wickedness in my
daughter's hollow eyes.
I hear your evil laugh when I hear her cries.
I feel your presence in her disappearing body.
I know that you want her soul.
But what you don't know is that I'm her Mother and a
mother's powers are stronger than the universe.
I will not let you destroy my daughter;
I will fight you to the end.
I will fight you until I win.
I know you as the devil.
The world knows you as "Anorexia."

-Janice Kieschnick,
written for Reader's Digest "100 Words or Less" contest.

"We take the good days from God, why not also the bad days?" Job 2:10 MSG

1. THE VIEW FROM THE MOUNTAIN TOP

"In the land of Uz there lived a man whose name was Job. This man was blameless and upright; he feared God and shunned evil. He was the greatest man among all the people of the East. One day the angels came to present themselves before the Lord, and Satan also came with them. The Lord said to Satan, "Where have you come from?" Satan answered the Lord, "From roaming through the earth and going back and forth in it." Then the Lord said to Satan, "Have you considered my servant Job? There is no one on earth like him; he is blameless and upright, a man who fears God and shuns evil." "Does Job fear God for nothing?" Satan replied. "Have you not put a hedge around him and his household and everything he has? You have blessed the work of his hands so that his flock and herds are spread throughout the land. But stretch out your hand and strike everything he has, and he will surely curse you to your face." The Lord said to Satan, "Very well, then, everything he has is in your hands, but on the man himself do not lay a finger." Then Satan went out from the presence of the Lord." (Job 1:1, 3, 6-12 NIV)

Although this book is not intended to portray my family as "modern day Job", I believe that God allowed Satan to enter our lives much the same way that God allowed Satan to enter the life of Job. If you would have told me a few years ago that the devil would show up at our front door, I would have laughed in your face! No way, I would have

15

argued! We are Christians--we go to church--we teach Sunday School--we pray. There's a big cross on the outside of our house. There are hundreds of crosses placed throughout our house. Why, we even have a stepping stone placed outside our back door that reads "As for me and my house, we will serve the Lord."

I didn't understand then that everything I just mentioned would not protect me from the evil of the devil, it just made for a bigger target. The devil doesn't waste his time and energy on the atheist protesting God on the street corner. He already has that person firmly in his grasp. Instead, Satan focuses on the people who openly love and praise God. "The enemy would not fight you if you didn't carry the ball. They try to tackle the one with the ball, not the one on the bench!"

Now picture for a moment the kind of family the devil might have his eyes on. You might picture the typical American family with three children, two dogs, one cat and a horse. The husband is a hard worker, who built a successful business with his own two hands. The wife is a "stay-at-home mom" who works part-time, so she's always available to volunteer for the kid's activities and to have chocolate chip cookies ready for after school.

The kids are good kids and healthy kids, who excel in school and sports and who love working with their 4-H animals. They live in a nice, brick, home, out in the country, with acres of land, a fishing pond, a swimming pool and lots of tall pine trees.

I just described our family, as seen from the mountain top, before God allowed anorexia to enter our lives. I sometimes would lay awake at night, think about how "lucky" we were and "pat myself on the back" for how successful we had become. I marveled at what a good job Trent and I had done in raising our children. People told us all the time what great kids we had raised.

Now if you're ready to close this book because you're sick of the dripping, sweetness of all the bragging, then join the crowd, because that's exactly how God felt! We never praised Him for all the gifts He had given us. We never thanked Him for our success or the success of our children, but we sure let Him know about the times we were disappointed in Him. We sure cursed Him and ignored Him when we didn't agree with situations in our lives. We sure blamed Him for everything bad that happened. What we didn't understand at that time is that nothing in our life is put there because of anything we have done on our own accord. Everything that we have or ever will have is a gift from God. As He can give gifts, He can also take away gifts. Everything is His will and He wants to know if we will praise Him and thank Him in good times and in difficult times. So as with a disrespectful, unruly, spoiled child who needs to be disciplined, God allowed Satan to enter our lives in the form of a terrible disease to see what our reaction would be, would we fall to our knees in repentance or turn our backs in rejection?

October 16, 2010

This weekend we went to visit Tanner at college. Looking around at the campus only reminds me that Katelyn's future is so uncertain! I don't know if she will be physically or emotionally ready to go away to college. I pray that God will reveal His plans for Katelyn to us! Sometimes I feel so lost and alone! God, are you there? Can you hear me?

April 11, 2011

Katelyn thinks she is gaining too much weight now and she is getting depressed and crying a lot and making our house miserable again! I don't know what to do other than just try and talk to her. Sometimes I feel like God has just stopped listening! I feel like we have been through so much and He just keeps putting more pain on us! I find myself not even wanting to pray anymore because I don't think He is listening! There are other people, who don't have to go through any trials in their life, so why do we have to go through so much?

"Even though I walk through the valley of the shadow of death, I will fear no evil, for you are with me; your rod and your staff, they comfort me." Psalm 23:4 NIV

2. THE JOURNEY THROUGH THE VALLEY

Nothing happens in our lives unless God allows it to happen. God is omnipresent. He is everywhere. He knows all. He sees all. He controls all. Our lives are planned by God before we are even born. "Before I formed you in the womb I knew you." (Jeremiah 1: 5 NIV) Everything that happens, good or bad, is planned by God. So if He approves it and allows it, then He surely has a reason for it, even if we don't understand it.

Because God is more powerful than Satan, the devil has no power in our lives unless God allows it. I can't tell you the exact time or day that demons entered our lives. I just know that God allowed Satan's demons to enter the mind of our daughter, through an illness, and after a year of battling the evil disease of anorexia and realizing that God is in full control, I can tell you that the demons are gone!

Our journey began in 2010 when our seventeen year old daughter, Katelyn was a junior in high school. She was feeling the burden and stress of four honors classes and of trying to remain in the number three academic position of her class. Also, she was feeling the pressure of keeping her already lean body in shape for cheerleading and softball. I took her to our family doctor for a yearly check-up and to discuss her high stress levels.

When she stepped on the scale that day, I had no indication that weight had become an issue to her. She was five foot, three inches tall and weighed 125 pounds, a healthy weight for an athlete. She had beautiful muscle tone and many people admired her build. We found it interesting to learn later that she hated her bulging muscles and would cringe if anyone asked her to flex her forearms to show her biceps.

After the doctor's checkup, on the way home in the car, she started to cry because of her weight. I tried to reason with her that she is beautiful and healthy, but she declared that she wanted to lose "just a little weight."

At first there weren't any drastic changes in her eating habits, just more healthy choices. Then one day, a comment was made in our community about the "fat cheerleaders" and that's all it took. The devil had reared his ugly head, diving into Katelyn's mind. People may wonder how a mother couldn't see the first signs of an eating disorder. In fact, people have asked me how I didn't see the signs at first. I can honestly say that an eating disorder doesn't happen overnight. It happens gradually, sometimes unnoticed until you are in the full swing of it, with your head spinning, wondering how you got there. You don't cure an eating disorder overnight either. It takes months and sometimes years for a full recovery. Sadly, some people who have an eating disorder will never make a full recovery.

Katelyn has always been a sensitive child; in the middle between an older brother, Tanner, and a younger sister, Landee. Growing up, she was a perfectionist and a "people pleaser", constantly striving to be perfect at everything she did, be it grades or sports or being the perfect daughter and sibling. She was always kind and polite to everyone.

20

Sometimes, I wondered if she was too polite because she would apologize to people for things that didn't need an apology. For instance, if her brother or sister took a toy away from her, she would apologize to them. She never wanted to give anyone a reason to dislike her. I tried to explain many times that no matter how nice we are to people, there will always be someone who will find fault in us. I think she was determined to prove that theory wrong. She never went through the "terrible two" stage, the defiant preteen years or the rebellious teenager phase. If her actions were anything less than perfect, then she thought maybe we wouldn't love her as much. So began the impossible task of trying to be perfect. And because no one is or ever will be perfect, this task began to destroy her body and her mind.

Over the next few months, she started eating healthier foods. This meant no soft drinks or tea, only fat free milk, lots of water, no sweets of any kind, no fried or greasy foods, no fast food, and always very careful choices at restaurants. Going to restaurants became a nightmare for our family, so we eventually stopped going.

Even though I didn't think that she needed to lose any weight, at first, I admired her will power. I thought to myself, "I wish I had her will power. I wish I had the will power to eat healthier and lose some weight." And so, I started dieting too, but little did I know that Katelyn was watching every move that I made. If I didn't eat breakfast or lunch, she thought it was okay to skip breakfast and lunch. If I ate only a salad for dinner, she thought it was okay to eat only a salad. I wish I knew then what I know now, that dieting and "being thin" are overrated when it costs your soul to achieve it.

21

Because she was a junior, she could leave the school's campus for lunch. We live too far away from the school, so she started going to a friend's house for lunch. I learned later from that friend's mother, that Katelyn never ate anything at their house. Also, around this time, she started jogging. "You know, Mom, softball playoffs are coming up soon and I have to stay in shape if we want to have a good season." Okay, I reasoned, jogging is good, maybe I will go with her sometime to walk while she jogs. Soon she became obsessed with exercise and if she missed a day without exercising, she would get really depressed. She even got up at 6:00 A.M. one morning and went jogging in the snow. I didn't know about this at the time, but I do now. We finally realized there was a major problem when one day she had a stomach virus and she still insisted that she needed to go jogging even though she felt terrible and weak. Of course, Trent and I put our foot down and said "No!", but she tried to sneak out of the house anyway and when we confronted her, she stormed to her room and cried herself to sleep. What had happened to our sweet daughter who never disobeyed us?

Katelyn's exercise program consisted of jogging for miles, swimming for hours, doing hundreds of sit-ups in her room in the middle of the night and when we started to monitor her exercising, we would hear her jogging-in-place in the shower. By now, school was out for the summer, but she had started to withdraw from her friends. Her life revolved around her "safe foods" which now consisted of fruits, vegetables, skim milk, salmon, pecans and lots of water. She avoided her "scary foods" which consisted of anything not just mentioned. She was consumed by calorie counting, cookbooks and cooking for the family, but she never ate anything that she cooked. If she wasn't on the computer searching for new recipes, then she was dividing her grapes and pecans into equal amounts of six per serving. If she wasn't exercising, then she was in her room crying.

Also, around the first of the summer, a routine dental checkup revealed that she needed all four of her wisdom teeth removed. After the surgery, the dentist advised us to give her only soft foods such as ice cream, pudding, yogurt or mashed potatoes for at least ten days. All of these foods scared her to death, so we managed to get her to drink "Slim Fast" drinks and in the process, she lost ten more pounds.

Her new phrase became "I don't understand...I don't understand why you think I have a problem. I don't understand why I can't exercise. I don't understand why I have to eat what everyone else is eating. I don't understand what's wrong with losing weight." Well, I didn't understand anything that was going on either, and I sure didn't understand what had happened to our once reasonable daughter, but I did know that she had an illness and that we needed help. More importantly, I knew that God understood and would provide an answer.

October 1, 2010

Five months into the "eating disorder." Five months into the nightmare. I woke up in the middle of the night, in a cold sweat. I sat up in bed thinking "It's almost flu season, if Katelyn gets a bad case of the flu, she will die!" I can't think like that. I have to put my full trust in God to heal her! That is my prayer every day!

She weighs 92 pounds now (she's lost 33 pounds) I walked into her room today as she was getting dressed. I couldn't look. I turned my head. She looks like a picture you would see of a person starving in a concentration camp. Where is my beautiful daughter?

Sometimes I feel like I am in mourning... mourning the loss of Katelyn before this disease entered her mind. Mourning the loss of her bubbly personality. Mourning the loss of her cheerful smile. Mourning the loss of her athletic ability. Mourning the loss of her chance to go to college. Mourning the loss of her future. God helps me through the day. God helps us as a family through the day. What do people do who don't know God?

October 3, 2010

We told Katelyn that we needed to start implementing a "scary food" into her diet once a week. Some type of food that she has restricted herself from eating. She can choose which food. She can't sleep. She is too worried about that "scary food". All she can think about is that "scary food." She decided maybe she would try some frozen yogurt, but when, when does she have to eat the yogurt? That worries her.

October 13, 2010

Katelyn had a good eating day today, but she panicked when she read the food journal that the dietician suggested I start keeping, and she realized I had put whole milk into her egg casserole. It's little things like this that set her back.

This illness has changed our whole family forever. I like to think that we have changed for the better, that we are closer to God. But I still worry about the lasting effects on Landee.

November 7, 2010

We went to church today and as usual Katelyn asked if she didn't have to eat as much today because she ate so much last night. She also asked if we could go straight home after church and have a small lunch. I said "yes" we will go home after church. But then at church, we got invited to go to a restaurant to celebrate her aunt's birthday. I felt like we needed to go for her birthday and Landee really wanted to go to spend time with the family. Katelyn said "NO" and pouted all through church. We decided to go to the restaurant and we told Katelyn that we would find something on the menu that she could eat.

Outside the restaurant, Katelyn started to cry. We finally went inside and ordered her a grilled chicken salad. As we talked and laughed, Katelyn eased up and she told me that she was sorry that she acted like a baby and that the salad was good. As we got ready to leave, her aunt hugged her and through tears said, "This is the best birthday present that you could have given me, coming to the restaurant and eating something even though it was so scary." Katelyn felt good about her decision and she was glad that she was able to do that for her aunt.

"Therefore what God has joined together, let man not separate." Matthew 19:6 NIV

3. MENDING THE BROKEN PIECES

Twenty-five years ago, on a chilly February day, in a candlelit church, I stood beside my future husband and vowed before God, our families and friends to "love, honor and cherish, forsaking all others, for better for worse, for richer, for poorer, in sickness and in health, to have and to hold, from this day forward, till death do us part." I wonder if any young couple, on their blissful wedding day, actually listens to or understands these vows? I wonder if any married couple can ever foresee the struggles their marriage will face while taking care of a sick child?

Trent and I were both blessed to have been raised in Christian homes by loving, Christian parents who took us to Sunday School and church. Growing up, we were both very active in our churches, getting involved in various youth group activities. After we were married, we knew the importance of going to church and raising our children in church. As a young married couple, we volunteered to be the Youth Leaders of our church for several years, taking the youth on ski trips, outings to amusements parks and lakes, and having weekly Bible studies. As we got older and had children of our own, we became involved in our kid's church activities, volunteering to help at all the fund raisers and to go on all the trips as chaperones. We have both served on many church boards and I have taught Sunday School and Vacation Bible School for almost twenty years. Our home was happy, our children were happy, and our marriage was good. But our marriage wasn't centered around God. We didn't pray together as a couple, we didn't pray together as a family. Our meal time prayers consisted of a memorized prayer from Trent's childhood. When I would ask him if he could just say a short prayer from his heart, he would grumble and say that his prayer was good enough. Trent wasn't the spiritual leader of the household that all fathers need to be, but, I reasoned, he is a good husband, a good father, a hard worker, and a good provider, so I'm not going to nag him about a meal time prayer. However, our marriage wasn't built on Christ's solid rock foundation, and with any shaky foundation, one crack might cause it to tumble to the ground and break into a million pieces. I have always heard that dealing with any stressful situation in a marriage "will either make it or break it." You will either become closer as a couple or you will be torn apart. I know for a fact that living with an anorexic child can cause a crack in a marriage's foundation especially when parents can't agree on the best type of treatment.

It's only human nature for mothers to be the compassionate, nurturing figure in a child's life, while fathers take on the strong, provider role. When a child is injured, most moms will rush to their aid, wipe away the tears and soothingly say "Let me kiss it and make it all better." On the other hand, most dads will glance their way and nonchalantly say "Get up, you're fine, big boys and girls don't cry." When a child skins a knee, both parents know exactly what to do. When a child has anorexia, parents have no clue what to do, but I have done enough research to know what I didn't want to do. If I could help it, so help me God, I would not send my daughter away to rehabilitation. I was listening to my heart, but Trent soon forgot about his heart's voice and began to listen to other people.

"So-and-so says that we have to send her to a rehab. So-and-so says a rehab is the only way she will ever get well. So-and-so says there was a person, who had a friend, who died of this disease. So-and-so says we are doing nothing and letting her die. So-and-so says we are being selfish by not sending her to a rehab." Well, my response to that was, so-and-so is not Katelyn's mother, and so-and-so has not witnessed, first hand, the terror in my daughter's eyes or hushed the voices in my daughter's head. I AM HER MOTHER. I will not abandon her when she needs me the most. If that's what so-and-so would do in this situation, then that's their business, but I need to at least try this new "Maudsley" program for the treatment of eating disorders that I had been researching and learning so much about. I fully agreed that at any given moment, if we saw that this program wasn't working, then we would try something else--even if that meant sending her to a rehab. I have never been a person that boldly states "It's my way or the highway," but on this issue, I was standing my ground and I desperately needed my husband's support. I had already told Trent that if he sent her away to a rehab without at least trying this new treatment program, then he better make arrangements with our local funeral home because that's where he would be sending me after I died of a broken heart.

Instead of turning this decision over to God, we began turning against each other. Instead of praying together as a couple, we began to argue all the time. Instead of talking rationally, we began to yell at each other. So one night, in the heat of an explosive argument, I calmly told Trent that if he couldn't support the decision to try the new program, then he needed to leave. Our number one priority was to help our daughter get well; I didn't have enough strength or energy to work on our marriage too. He never actually left, he just never came home. He poured himself into his job, often spending the night at his welding shop, because that was the only thing that kept him sane and eased the pain of the problems at home.

No one knew we were having marital problems, not even our kids. They had been through enough. They didn't need another burden, especially Katelyn, who would have blamed herself. There was already enough gossip around town about our sick daughter, we didn't need more gossip about our failing marriage. So, we suffered in silence. We didn't even confide in our Pastor, who would have gladly and eagerly counseled with us. It was almost as if nothing else mattered in the world, except keeping our daughter alive--even if that meant letting our marriage die. The devil already knew how much easier it would be to attack our family if we were apart.

For a brief period during the summer of 2010, we walked through this valley, separated and alone, instead of hand in hand with each other and God. We forgot the vows we had made so many years ago, we forgot about "in sickness and in health." Then one night, in late July, Trent was asleep on our couch, exhausted and alone, when he had a vision. It was like an out-of-body experience because he was awake, but in a trance and his body was momentarily paralyzed. In his vision, he was all alone in a dark room and somewhere in the distance, he could hear the horrific cries of his family and he could see vague shadows of someone beating us to death with a baseball bat. He recognized our voices as we pleaded for mercy, he heard our bones being shattered, and he saw the blood. He wanted desperately to help us, but he couldn't move. He tried to scream for help, but no sound came from his mouth. He tried to cover his ears to muffle the sound of our moans and as our cries grew silent, the attacker found him. With one harsh blow to his head, he knew it would soon be over.

For the first time in his life, he felt helpless and hopeless. He envisioned that he was in hell and the devil was the one attacking us. There was literally nothing he could do to save his family. When the trance ended, his heart was racing and he was dripping with sweat. He knew that this vision was from God, telling him that as long as he tried to handle everything by himself, he would be helpless and hopeless. He knew he needed to turn his life completely over to God and become the spiritual leader of our house. He immediately fell to his knees, begging God to show him how to be the Godly father and husband that he needed, and wanted, to be.

The next day, with tears in his eyes and a tremble in his voice, he shared his vision with me. As we embraced each other and cried together, he asked me to forgive him for all the years we spent without Christ as the center of our marriage. Now, more than ever, we needed each other and we needed God to help us get through this crisis. As a baby learning to crawl, Trent became a new creation; the old ways were gone, never to return again. He began to delve eagerly in the Bible, absorbing everything he read. He began to say long, meaningful prayers, coming straight from his heart. He began to pray for me and our children. We began to pray together as a couple, as a family and we began to have daily Bible devotions. He began to share the Bible, his life changing experience, and his relationship with God to anyone and everyone who will listen.

Our marriage became stronger than ever before and we began to cling to each other because it seemed as if the whole world was against us. Then late one evening, I was looking for Trent, but I couldn't find him anywhere. I just needed to feel his presence after a long day of fighting the demons. I searched the entire house and then went outside to the barn. He always enjoys the peacefulness and sounds of the barn animals, but he wasn't there either. I began to panic and to dwell on negative thoughts…had the toll of dealing with this disease on a daily basis became too much for him to bear?

Once more, I hurried through the house and then something caught my eye. In our dark bedroom, off in the corner, Trent was kneeling by our bed, reading the Bible, using only the illumination from his lighted, reading glasses. As he glanced up, he didn't even have to explain. I already knew that reading the Bible and prayer had become the only access to calmness and peace during this storm in our lives.

Trent will be the first person to tell you that he wouldn't wish for anyone to go through a year like what we went through. He would never wish the disease of anorexia on any family, but he is so grateful that God allowed us to go through this trial because it brought us to our knees in prayer and brought us closer together as a couple and a family. We were blind, but now our eyes have been opened to the wonderful grace of our loving God, who healed our daughter and healed our marriage.

December 24, 2010

I am so thankful for Trent that he is patient and understanding about my mood swings and my depression and that he is closer to God than ever before in his life! There is nothing more powerful than a praying husband and father!

January 7, 2011

Trent and I had a long talk tonight. Sometimes I find myself shutting down and not wanting to talk to him about my feelings or concerns. He is trying so hard to be understanding. We talked about how we literally surrendered Katelyn over to God before she started getting better.
This brought us to our knees in prayer and we said to God, "Here she is Lord-she is yours-take her from us if that is your plan." Just like Abraham and his son Isaac, God knew that we were willing to let her go. And with that prayer, an enormous peace came over Trent and me and we were ready for God's will.

"I was sick and you looked after me...I tell you the truth, whatever you did for one of the least of these brothers of mine, you did for me." Matthew 25:36 & 40 NIV

4. THE POWER OF A MOTHER'S LOVE

Several years ago, when our kids were little, we raised a small herd of cattle. Being the "city girl" that I am, I absorbed and treasured every aspect of this country life. Every day, I would take the kids with me to check on the cows, sometimes twice a day during calving season. All three of our children have witnessed the miracle of a new life coming into the world by watching these mother cows give birth to their calves. We marveled at every new calf that was born, with their wobbly legs, ready to take on the world. We named each new calf, and somehow we felt a special bond with each one, but I always kept Trent's warning in my mind, "Never get between a momma cow and her calf. She will do anything to protect her baby!" I know exactly how a momma cow feels. I will do anything to protect my children.

Webster's dictionary defines "intuition" as a quick insight, recognized immediately without a reasoning process. (1) A "mother's intuition" is much more powerful than this. Almost every mother will tell you that she has a special sense about knowing what is right for her children and her family. Some believe that mothers have a bond so strong with their children that they have a way of knowing when their child is at risk. Unfortunately, many mothers have been trained to ignore this sense, trusting that educational experts and child psychologists know more than they do. It is possible to gain a lot of knowledge from experts, but no one is more likely to love a child as much as the child's mother or father. The parents are uniquely qualified to be the expert on what is best for the child. (2)

When Katelyn became sick, we immediately started looking for ways to help her. I read over twenty books about eating disorders and spent thousands of hours on the internet researching for the best possible types of treatment. We inquired about in-patient rehabilitation centers; we made phone calls to these centers; we talked to several parents, who had children with eating disorders, about the advantages and disadvantages of sending Katelyn to an in-patient rehabilitation center and we prayed about it.

We felt that we knew our daughter better than anyone else and we knew that Katelyn's body and mind were too fragile to be sent away from home, for months, all alone in a hospital, maybe thousands of miles away. In all of her life, she had never even been away to an overnight camp. My niece, who has also struggled with an eating disorder, begged us not to send Katelyn to an in-patient rehabilitation center. She spent three months at one, coming out more enriched in the disease, and she didn't think that was the right choice for Katelyn.

So we decided as a family that our house would become Katelyn's rehab. Trent, myself, Tanner and Landee would be her treatment team. It would take all of us, God and doctors, but we would help her get better. We knew her better than anyone, we loved her more than anyone, and we would not send her away to strangers as if we were abandoning her. Call it "mother's intuition" because I knew in the deepest part of my heart that we had made the right

35

decision, but not everyone felt the same way. Statements were made, such as, "You are too close to the situation to see how sick she really is. Everyone else can see that she is dying, you are just in denial. You are more concerned about her finishing her senior year than finishing her life." Really? I carried this child in my body for nine months; I took care of her when she had chicken pox and strep throat; I mended her wounded knees and soothed her wounded heart; I have lived with her and loved her for seventeen years and you're telling me that I don't know she's really sick? Never underestimate the power of a mother's love!

I'm not saying that in-patient rehabilitation clinics are bad or wrong. I know there are some very good clinics in this country. I'm just saying that it wasn't the right decision for us. Through all of my research, I found a program that caught my attention. It's called the "Maudsley Family Based Therapy" (3) treatment for eating disorders and it's just that, family based. The concept is that a child with an eating disorder has a better chance of getting well faster and staying well if they are treated in a family environment. Statistics show that this type of treatment is 90% more effective than other types of treatment. Some studies even suggest that people with eating disorders, who are placed in in-patient rehabs, are so traumatized by the experience, that they will gain weight fast just to be able to go home. Once they are home, they are more prone to have a relapse because the mental issues were not resolved. (4)

The "Maudsley" program involves a team made up of a medical doctor, a therapist, a dietician, and the immediate family, all working together, on the same page, for the benefit of the child. The child must be able to trust all of them and know that they are all working toward the same goal, to get the child well.

We began the "Maudsley Family Based Therapy" treatment program in August 2010. At the start of this program Katelyn had lost 40 pounds, now weighing 85 pounds. This program consisted of weekly visits to our family doctor, who charted Katelyn's weight progress, requested extensive medical tests on a monthly basis and monitored her anti-anxiety medication. He was her doctor since she was three years old. She knew him, she trusted him, and he had all of her life-long medical records. The program also consisted of weekly visits to a therapist, who focused on her mental state, and weekly visits to a dietician, who monitored her diet. The therapist and the dietician told us that Katelyn didn't meet the criteria level needed to be placed in an in-patient rehab. Based on the "Level of Care Criteria for Patients with Eating Disorders" (5) which through the patient's medical records, medical complications, weight, and psychology records and mental state, rank the patient from level one to level five. Level one means the patient needs out-patient therapy, such as with the "Maudsley" program and level five means the patient needs immediate hospitalization. As of September 1, 2010, Katelyn was placed at a level one and she never progressed past that level.

It was difficult trying to schedule all of these appointments around school and school activities, but we managed, even if it meant having a doctor's appointment early before school started or during her lunch break. We were so thankful that the school counselor allowed Katelyn to have a free period in the morning and another free period after lunch because in a year, we would go to over 80 doctor's visits, but it was well worth it. In addition to these weekly doctor's visits, Katelyn also met weekly with a family friend, who had suffered with anorexia and bulimia when she was younger. This friend was a pastor's wife in our town and she had been an Olympic swimmer who had to give up her dreams of competitive swimming due to these illnesses. No one could possibly know what goes through an anorexic's mind than someone who has also lived through it.

The "Maudsley" program also centered on the entire family getting involved with the "re-feeding process" which is known as Phase One. Meal time around our house during this phase was not pleasant. We all became frustrated. I have to admit that there were times when Trent and Landee would leave the dinner table without finishing their meal, and there were times when I wanted to give up completely, but I knew Katelyn needed me. I spent hours in the grocery store trying to find new foods that I thought she might eat. I spent hours preparing and cooking meals because she had to eat a certain amount of calories and servings from each food group. I kept a food journal to show the dietician what Katelyn had eaten, and each week the dietician would increase the calorie intake and each week this caused new frustrations. A few months into the program, the dietician told us to start implementing a "scary" food into her meal plan every week. This needed to be a food which Katelyn hadn't allowed herself to eat in a long time. She could choose what food, but my job was to make sure she actually ate what she had chosen. After many sleepless nights worrying about it, her first "scary" food choice was frozen yogurt. Spoonful after spoonful was eaten through clinched teeth. She was frustrated and angry that we were making her eat something that scared her to death.

It would sometimes take over an hour for Katelyn to eat one meal because her stomach had become so small. It was painful to her body to eat large amounts of food. I had to stay with her at every meal and I would sit beside her, rub her back and encourage her as tears rolled down her face. I would try to distract her by talking about everyday events and this would sometimes help to get her mind off of the food sitting in front of her that she had to eat before she could leave the table. Soon, she started hiding uneaten portions of food by putting it in a napkin and throwing it away. She had convinced herself that I wouldn't notice. This was the only way she could escape her fear of the food without disappointing me. So, I had to convince her numerous times that food was her "medicine." I had to gently, but persistently make her understand that without her "medicine" she could die.

I would tell her that if she had another disease, such as cancer, she would have to take medication to help her get well. She might not want to take the medicine, it might taste bad, or hurt her stomach, or have side effects, but it was inevitable to her health and life. Much like coaxing a small child to take the spoonful of "yucky" medicine, I had to keep drilling this into her head, "food is your medicine, medicine is good, without it, you will die!"

This was our daily life for six months. This was our "new normal" and an example of a "normal" afternoon would sound something like this:

When Katelyn would come home from school each day, I knew the peacefulness of the afternoon was over. When I would hear her car drive into the driveway, I would take a deep breath and hold it for a few seconds before slowly letting it out. I had to mentally prepare myself for who would be walking through the door. Would it be sweet, bubbly Katelyn, who would greet me cheerfully, or would it be the "other" Katelyn, who would come through the door in tears? Sometimes, it would be the "stressed out" Katelyn, who was sullen, with a worried look on her thin face. I would brace myself for the worst and follow her into her bedroom. In my hand would be her afternoon snack, as I braced myself for the battle. She would look at the snack with disgust and roll her eyes. I, on the other hand, would think the snack looked very appetizing, two graham crackers, sandwiched together with yogurt. I had frozen it to make it similar to an ice cream sandwich and I knew that it would melt soon, becoming less appealing to her than it already was.

I would sit the oversized plate down on her desk and gently tell her for the umpteenth time that she knew she had to eat her afternoon snack. The huge plate would make the food appear smaller, another crafty trick that I had learned. By now, the frustrated Katelyn would make her appearance. "I don't want a snack," she would wail, "I just ate lunch a few hours ago and I feel gross!" And then the tears would start as she would confide in me the stress of the day. She might be worried about an upcoming test. She just knew she would never be able to study enough for the test. She just knew she would fail it and the teacher would think she was stupid. It wasn't unusual for spiteful words to be spewed from her mouth. "I hate school! I hate tests! I hate that you are making me eat so much food! You just want me to be fat! I hate myself! Please, just go away!"

I knew this wasn't Katelyn talking, I knew it was the demon. I had to try really hard to separate the illness from my precious daughter. This would be a typical day. She would eventually eat the snack. It might take a while and I might have to throw it away and make a fresh one, but that was minor compared to the major step of her eating it. Her tears would stop, for a while and she would be in a better mood, as she apologized a hundred times for what she had said earlier. She would study for the test and not only pass it, but make a perfect score. You see, she had to, because in her mind, she had to be perfect.

Now came the time for Phase Two. In January 2011, after Katelyn had gained fifteen pounds, the dietician said it was time to give Katelyn some control. This was the part of the "Maudsley" plan that allowed Katelyn to be in control of her own eating. This was also the time that the weekly doctor, dietician and therapist visits were decreased to twice a month and then eventually once a month. We knew that this would be the most difficult step, but it would also be the first step needed toward her independence. She would be allowed to eat what she wanted, when she wanted, and to keep the food journal herself. I was instructed to give her freedom and to "not say a word" when the choices that she made didn't seem to have enough calories in them. I was also instructed to let the dietician know if she started skipping meals. This part of the program was very frustrating because even though Katelyn knew that she needed the extra calories, it was very difficult for her mind to accept that she was letting her body control this. An example of this was when she saw some cheese in the grocery store one day. She loved it, but hadn't allowed herself to eat it in a long time. She asked if we could buy that cheese. "Sure, just get the kind that you want and put it in the shopping cart," I said. She stood there, staring at the cheese, reaching for it several times, but then always pulling her hand back. She couldn't pick up the cheese. I had to pick up the cheese and put it in the basket. You see, her body was telling her that she could have it, but her mind was telling her that if she actually picked it up, then she would have no self-control. If I picked it up, put it in the cart, paid for it and then served it to her, only then was it okay for her to eat it. Oh, the games that the devil plays in our minds!

For a whole year, from August 2010 until August 2011, our lives centered around the "Maudsley Family Based Therapy" program, eventually beginning Phase Three. We tried to return to normal life, which meant no more doctors' visits and no more journal-keeping. By now, Katelyn had regained all of her weight, had overcome many obstacles in her life, and was living like a normal young adult and preparing to leave for college in the fall.

Sometime during this blur of a year, I received a phone call from my niece; the one I mentioned earlier who also struggled with an eating disorder. She was so amazed at Katelyn's progress and she wanted to tell me that she was proud I had listened to my "mother's intuition" by helping Katelyn to get well at home and not sending her off to a rehab. She told me she wished her parents would have known about the "Maudsley" program when she had been sick. Her parents are good parents. They tried to help their daughter the best way they knew how, but they didn't know about this program, and that is when I realized that I needed to somehow tell the world about our experience.

I don't want to be discouraging in any way, but everyone needs to be aware that this program isn't easy. It is demanding on the entire family's time, energy, patience and finances, but Katelyn is living proof that it's well worth the effort put into it. This program also requires one parent to be with the child at every meal for at least six months and for one parent to be able to take the child to all the doctor, therapist and dietician appointments. In our family's situation, this person was me. Trent and I are both self-employed, him as a welder and myself as a bookkeeper and real estate agent. We decided that his income was too valuable for our family to give up, so he continued to work while I cut back on my hours. I am so thankful that God allowed us to go through this healing process side by side with Katelyn, that God allowed steady jobs to come to Trent to help pay the medical expenses and that God sent this program to us. My prayer is that God will open eyes, hearts and minds to the healing that can begin through His power and through the power of not just a mother's love, but also a family's love.

October 7, 2010

We went to see the doctor this morning for Katelyn's weekly check-up. She's been doing so good with her eating and her food thoughts. We were really excited to see some positive results-

weight gain. She stepped on the scales and the nurse said that she had lost five more pounds. How could this be? I cried right there in the doctor's office. He said that she had to gain weight by the next appointment. Trent keeps telling me to be patient and wait on the Lord. I WANT HER WELL NOW! I WILL NOT let her go off to a rehab! Am I such a bad mother for wanting to help her get better at home with her family? When she came home for lunch today, we talked about how we would have to get more calories in her diet. She climbed up into my lap like a two year old and cried, "This is going to be so hard mommy!" This coming from a seventeen year old senior who should be becoming independent and getting ready for college!

October 20, 2010

Today is my birthday and I wanted to wake up today and for it to be a "normal" day. Our family doesn't have "normal" days anymore, but I am thankful today. I am thankful that I have one more day to "re-feed" Katelyn. Trent reminded me that it could be so much worse. We could have a child fighting for its life in a cancer hospital. I know I'm being selfish to want everything to be normal again. I just wish I knew when this would end!

"Avoid godless chatter, because those who indulge in it will become more and more ungodly." 2 Timothy 2:16 NIV

5. ANOREXIA CANNOT TAKE OUR LOVE

Anorexia can take so many things away from you.....
It can take your health
It can take your spirit
It can take your personality
It can take your smile
It can take your dreams
It can take your joy
It can take your goals
It can take your future
It can take your athletic ability
It can take your hope
It can take your friends
It can take your family
It can take your body
It can take your muscles
It can take your heart
It can take your appetite
It can take your innocence
But, anorexia cannot take away our love for each other and our faith in God!

Written in my journal
October 2010

We live in a small, north Texas town, and one of the unfortunate benefits of living in a small town is that you hear all the rumors. The conversations at the local coffee shops all center around the latest rumors; who's having an affair; who's getting a divorce; who's teenage daughter is pregnant; whose teenage son got drunk last weekend. I have to admit, I used to join in on all these conversations and I have contributed to my share of the gossip and the rumors. That was until my anorexic daughter became the center of those hurtful rumors and I asked God to help me stop gossiping and spreading rumors.

The first thing I wanted to do was scream every time I heard a new rumor about Katelyn. "Have you seen that anorexic girl? She's just doing that for attention!" "The only reason that cheerleader is losing so much weight is because she wants to be the skinniest flyer on the squad." "Have you heard she weighs seventy pounds now?" "You know she throws up!" "She wears Invisaligners (invisible braces) because her teeth are rotting out." "Her parents won't get her help because they don't want her to miss her senior year."

The second thing that I wanted to do was to punch the people who started those rumors. And believe me, living in a small town, you know who says what. But, then I realized that I would be wasting a lot of energy punching a lot of ignorant people, and I wouldn't be of any help to Katelyn if I were in jail, so the only thing left to do was to try to educate people about what anorexia really is.

Before this disease entered our lives, I hadn't paid too much attention to it, and, yes, it is a disease. I have had people tell me, even family members, that it isn't a disease.

"All she has to do is eat and she will get better."

"Just lock her in her room, when she gets hungry enough, she'll want to eat."

46

"Let her come live with me for a week, I'll fix her!"

"It's all her fault. She did this to herself."

Shame on the people who don't know all the facts, but voice their opinion anyway. After months of research and living with an anorexic, I am here to tell you-YES, IT IS A DISEASE, a terrible mental disease that a person does not "choose." Anorexia "chooses" you!

Anorexia is not reserved for "spoiled little rich kids" starving for attention as portrayed by the media today. It is NOT caused by over-controlling parents, rejection by parents, low self-esteem or low self-worth, as a Christian speaker once said on her radio broadcast. It can strike anyone, at any age, any gender, and any nationality.

Anorexia Nervosa is the Latin word translated to mean "nervous loss of appetite." Anorexics do not have an appetite, just as many people experience a lack of appetite when recovering from a stomach virus.

Some studies suggest that anorexia is genetic, a trait passed down from generation to generation. It is one of medicine's biggest mysteries, with 75 out of 1,000,000 being diagnosed. It is also one of the deadliest and misunderstood of mental illnesses. Twenty percent of anorexics will die. Of that number, half will die from medical complications, the other half from suicide. More than 1,000 people will die this year from anorexia in the United States. Only four out of ten with anorexia will make a full recovery. (6)

Just like with any disease, a person doesn't choose to have cancer, a person doesn't choose to have diabetes, a person doesn't choose to have anorexia. As strange as this may sound, just think about it for a minute. The average person can't go very long without food. If we do, we get weak and light-headed. Our bodies tell us that we have to eat food soon. Anorexics, on the other hand, are just the opposite; they get stronger, feel more alive and can endure long periods of no food without feeling the effects. One study even suggests that hundreds of years ago when there were nomadic tribes, some members in the tribe were sent out to look for food. They could endure long stretches of having no food. They thrived very well on no food while they traveled hundreds of miles in search of food that their tribe desperately needed to survive. The rest of the tribe became lethargic and had to conserve their energy until food could be found and brought back to the camp. Could this, in fact, be the first realization of prehistoric anorexia? (7)

Early diagnosis and treatment can improve the odds of recovery by a large percentage. Knowing the facts about anorexia will help family, friends and providers to recognize the signs and symptoms. Signs of anorexia include: an intense drive for thinness; fear of becoming fat; distorted body image; excessive exercising; a perfectionist personality; preoccupation with food, cooking, nutrition and calories; avoiding situations where food is involved; social withdrawal; emotional changes such as irritability, depression, anxiety; developing rituals about preparing and eating food; and restrictions not only to food, but also to relationships, social activities and other pleasures. (8)

If left untreated, anorexia can result in serious medical conditions such as: low blood pressure; low heart rate; reduced bone density; muscle loss and weakness; dehydration resulting in kidney failure; dry brittle hair and skin; excessive growth of "soft downy" hair on body; retarded growth; intolerance to cold, and lack of abnormal menstrual flow. Proper medical treatment involving physicians, psychiatric professionals, family, friends play an important role in the success of the person who has anorexia. (9)

Anorexia also affects the most important organ of the body—the brain. Starvation of the body also starves the brain and can lead to depression. When Cortisol (a hormone released into the body) runs out due to abnormal levels of stress and the rest of the body is depleted, a sickness response occurs; fatigue, impaired cognition, sleep disturbances, anorexia, and depressed mood can occur. (10)

Go to any internet search website and type in the word "anorexia" and you will be overwhelmed with the facts and statistics that you find. You may be shocked, you may not understand, you may not believe what you read, you may be sympathetic or you may not even care. Now, actually live with an anorexic and you WILL become their protector, their voice, their strength, their help, and their advocate to the entire world who misunderstand and misjudge this illness.

I recently watched an afternoon television talk show about the effects of anorexia on a family. I watched in amazement and disbelief as the well-known host, who everyone in the world admires and respects, belittled and degraded the anorexic young lady being interviewed, while she sobbed with her face hidden in her hands. Wow, the ever so influential power of a well-known person who knows nothing about the subject, but who wants to keep the television ratings up. I don't have that kind of power, but I do have what I know and what I lived! No one would ever tell a parent of a child with cancer, that because they are doing everything in their power to save that child's life, they are "rewarding bad behavior" because that child is sick and "ignoring good behavior" in other siblings. That talk show host said that about anorexia. When a child is sick, whether it be with anorexia, bulimia, cancer, diabetes, or any other disease, parents will do everything that they can to help their child. It isn't an easy road, it's a long and tiring process and it does affect the whole family. In our case, Katelyn received the type of treatment that she needed and she made a full recovery.

She knows without a shadow of a doubt that we love her so much that we went through this healing process with her, side by side. We didn't abandon her. We didn't give up on her. We didn't send her away. As for Tanner and Landee, they were involved in the treatment process also, and they know that we love them just as much as Katelyn and would do the same for them in any situation.

October 9, 2010

Katelyn was in the bathroom. I heard her "gasp." I ran to the bathroom to see if everything was alright. For the first time she said, "Oh my goodness, Mom! I look like a skeleton!" Thank you, God, for this little bit of realization!

October 15, 2010

I went to the Pep Rally today. It took every ounce of strength I had to get out of the car. I sat in my car and cried, begging God to please make the pain go away. I don't want to hurt anymore. I don't want to cry anymore. It's so hard watching Katelyn cheer, and seeing her bones in the cheer outfit-- seeing that she can't jump anymore because she's lost her muscles. It is hard knowing that everyone is talking about her. I go because she needs me there. After the Pep Rally, we went to the Sonic to talk before she had to go back to school. She told me, "Mom, I feel like I'm in a dream. I feel like I'm dreaming that I have anorexia. How did this happen to me?" I told her one day we will wake up out of this dream.

October 18, 2010

It was a good day! Thank You, Lord for another pound gained! Tonight at our daily Bible devotion we talked about "Inner Beauty" and how we need to let Jesus shine through us so that we are beautiful inside and out. We asked God to give us the words that we need to say to people who asks us about Katelyn. We pray that one day we will be able (with the help of God) to help someone else who may be going through something like this.

November 26, 2010

Big Step!!!!!! Katelyn got up hungry today! She wanted to make her own breakfast. She hasn't touched food to make it herself in over five months. She made a yogurt, cereal, fruit, and walnut parfait and ate the whole thing. She had so much fun making her own food that she made all of her meals today! Thank You Lord!

January 4, 2011

After school today, Landee turned on the T.V., and there was a famous actress who had battled anorexia. She had written a book and she was telling her story. Katelyn sat there glued to the T.V. She couldn't believe what the actress was saying. Katelyn kept asking, "Did I look like that?" after we saw a picture of the actress when she weighed 82 pounds with her bones sticking out. We said "yes, you looked like that when you weighed 85 pounds." She kept saying, "But that actress is beautiful, how could she not see how beautiful she is?" We asked, "How could you not see how beautiful you are?" As the actress described what her family went through, Katelyn kept saying "Landee, I'm so sorry that you had to go through that!"

"Fear not, for I am with thee; be not dismayed; for I am thy God…" Isaiah 41:10 KJV

6. FEAR NOT

A speaker on a Christian radio station once said that there are 365 "fear not" in the Bible, one for every day of the year.(11) I haven't actually counted, but I do know that God tells us many times in the Bible "Fear not" (Matthew 1:20, Luke 1:13, Luke 2:10, Luke 12:32 KJV)

Even though we have this assurance right in front of us, written in the Bible, the devil still has a way of sneaking into our minds, whispering in our ear and planting fear into our hearts. There is nothing that the devil loves more than for Christians to worry and be afraid and to forget that God is in control.

There are many forms of fear: fear of failure, fear of rejection, fear of loss, fear of heights, fear of germs, fear of crowds, fear of enclosed spaces and the list goes on. My youngest daughter, Landee, has a fear of germs. If only I had been smart enough to invent "Germ X," I would be a millionaire. She has a bottle of the stuff in her room, on her key chain, in her backpack, in her gym bag, in the car, and in my purse. She never leaves home without it.

I have a fear of elevators. Call it "claustrophobia," call it "cowardly," call it "stupid," I don't care what you call it, I literally panic at having to get in an elevator. You might ask, "What's the big deal? The doors open, you get in, you push the buttons, the doors close and you go to the next floor." Well, I'm just fine up until the doors close and then I panic. My heart begins to beat faster, my mind races, I can't breathe, and I can't think of anything else except getting out of there fast! This fear is very real to me and unless you have ever experienced a fear of elevators, you can never fully understand my fear. The solution to my fear is that I avoid elevators. I have convinced myself that taking the stairs is healthier anyway. My mother has suffered for many years of her life with the fear of crowds and being around a lot of people. Her fear was so strong that we spent most of my childhood avoiding large crowds. Anytime we went places, such as to church or school programs, we always sat in the back near an exit so we could leave in a hurry if she had a panic attack. The solution to her fear was to avoid crowds and people altogether. She became a prisoner in her own home because of this fear. It took over fifty years for my mom to find a doctor who understood her fear and could help her to overcome it. This fear was very real to her and no one can begin to understand the power of this fear unless you have actually lived it.

Katelyn had a fear of food and unlike elevators and crowds, no one can avoid food, but she tried. She literally panicked at the thought of eating certain foods. This is a major characteristic of anorexics; the devil tells them that food is poison to their bodies. The calories, the fat, the salt, the sugar, the flour are all bad, and so anorexics become experts at knowing exactly how many calories, how much fat, how many carbohydrates, how much protein is in anything they eat. Because of this fear, they eat very little. This illustrates how anorexics are normal in every other aspect of their lives, excelling in school and athletics, but crumbling under this intense fear of food. I could tell you about Katelyn's fear of food until I was blue in the face, but you could never understand unless you had actually witnessed it.

One afternoon, my sister-in-law stopped by the house to see if she could do anything to help out, such as bring us dinner for our meal that night. She made a suggestion of getting Subway sandwiches and then she saw the terror in Katelyn's eyes. She is one of only a few who actually witnessed the devil at work in Katelyn's mind.

Another day, my mom and I were going to one of Landee's basketball games. We were talking about Katelyn and I was describing to her Katelyn's fear of food and how hard it has been trying to convince her that food isn't the enemy. She commented that she just couldn't understand how anybody could be afraid of food. I've heard that comment a million times from people who don't understand. "Food is good," she said, "God gave us food and appetites and taste buds so that we could enjoy food, and food makes us healthy and strong." I replied, "All true, but Mom, do you remember when you used to have panic attacks and you couldn't be around people so you just stayed home? Do you remember what that felt like? Close your eyes for a minute and think back to that dark time in your life. You didn't understand it, Dad didn't understand, no one understood it, but that fear controlled your life. Can you relive that time in your mind right now? Can you relive how real that fear was and how much it engulfed your life?" She slowly opened her eyes and looked at me in amazement and said, "I didn't understand until you described it that way, but now I do!"

October 1, 2010

    Katelyn was invited to a birthday party tonight. She didn't want to go. I told her that she needed to go because it's for one of the friends who has been nice to her. "Mom, I'm scared to go! Why do I have to go? They will be eating steak. Do I have to eat steak? If I don't eat, they will all start talking about me again, they will start rumors again!" I told her that she needed to go to the party and at least try to eat what they were serving. She had a panic attack before she left. She sat on the couch and cried. We said a prayer together, and after she left, I texted her a Bible verse, "I can do all things through Christ who strengthens me." (Philippians 4:13 NIV)

    Later, she texted me back, "I did it Mom, I ate in front of them. I chose chicken instead of steak, but I had two servings of salad! I did it Mom! Are you proud of me?" Yes, I am proud of you and I love you and God will help us get through this!

October 2, 2010

    Today was a good day! It's Saturday, so no school, no being around people who don't understand. Katelyn and I spent all day together decorating the house for fall. Landee is gone all weekend to a church retreat. We went to Wal-Mart to buy pumpkins and decorations. We went to the candy aisle to get Halloween candy. Katelyn had been happy all day, but now she's quiet. I could see

56

the torment on her face. I asked her what was wrong. She looked terrified of something. I looked around to see if someone else was in the aisle with us. No, it's just us. Then I realized, it's the candy, she's scared of the candy. She looked at a package of "Dove Chocolate" candy. This used to be her favorite candy. She wanted to buy a package and take it home, she wanted so desperately to eat some candy, but she can't. She won't let herself. "Maybe another day," she said. "I know I will get better someday." She walked away from the candy aisle. I pray "someday" will come soon!

October 31, 2010

Today was our church picnic. We all used to love the church picnic with all the food and games. Then Katelyn said that she didn't want to go, But I said, "WE ARE GOING!" I brought along some of her "safe" foods: grapes, carrots, pecans, whole wheat bread. I told her that I would fix her a plate with only things that I knew she would eat and then she could fix me a plate. She sat her plate down at the table, but she didn't eat. She went to the dessert table and got tons of ice cream and cobbler for everyone at our table, but none for her. The counselor said this is so others won't watch what she eats. I didn't make a scene in front of everybody about her not eating her food. Then she went to play Bingo. She tried desperately all afternoon to win a plate of cupcakes. I don't know why, she would

57

never eat cupcakes.

November 6, 2010

    Today we went to a wedding. It's nice to have a reason to celebrate and be happy. Of course, we always have the cloud looming over our heads of what Katelyn will eat (if she will eat anything at all). Katelyn and Landee were servers at the wedding, so they spent a lot time in the kitchen. My mom told me that she saw Katelyn eating boiled shrimp and fruit. Later, I saw her eating a piece of wedding cake. She didn't know that I was watching her. Then, I saw the look of disgust on her face as she realized that she had given in to her temptation. When we got home, Trent found her jogging in place in her room.

December 21, 2010

    Tanner is home from college and it's always been our family tradition to drive to the city and see the Christmas light display and then eat at a nice restaurant. We were all excited and as we rode in the car, we were all talking and laughing. It's nice to have Tanner home. The kids talked about going to the mall to get me something special for Christmas. When we got to the restaurant, the conversation was light, and then the waiter came to take our order. Katelyn said that she wasn't going to order anything because she wasn't hungry. I argued with her that she had to eat something nutritious to stay on her balanced diet, but she refused and said "You get on my nerves!" So I told her "You get on ALL of our nerves!" She got up and stormed to the bathroom. The whole night seemed ruined. As she was gone, Landee said, "Doesn't she care that if she doesn't eat, someone will come take me away?" When she came back to the table, she sat there and watched us eat. Everyone ate their meal in silence. You could see the look in Tanner's eyes. He wished that he could go back to college and get away from all of this. But this is our daily life now and we can't get away. As bad as I want to, I can't run away.

I told the kids that we weren't going to the mall now because I didn't want a gift. I wanted to scream, "All I want for Christmas is to have a normal family again!"

January 10, 2011

Katelyn went to the grocery store with me today. She was in a cooking mood and she wanted to make dinner for our family. The good part about this is that now she will eat what she makes, as long as it is healthy. In the store, we walked down the baby food aisle and I laughed (I can laugh about it now) because I remembered when I was trying so desperately to get her to eat anything and one day she said that a certain baby food looked good , so I

59

wanted to buy it if she would eat it. Then I talked about how she used to always eat hot peppers and hot salsa because she had read somewhere that these foods would help her burn more calories. She didn't remember doing any of this. Maybe not remembering is her way of shutting out the memories and the pain.

"After all, no one ever hated his own body, but he feeds and cares for it, just as Christ does the church…" Ephesians 5:29 NIV

7. THERE'S NO SUCH PLACE AS PERFECTVILLE

Once upon a time, there was a beautiful girl with a beautiful smile. She was a good athlete, with strong muscles. Every day she thanked God for everything that He had given her.

One day, she looked in the mirror and decided that she didn't like what she saw. "I'm ugly," she cried! "I'm fat and my teeth are crooked and my face has too many pimples and my hair isn't long enough!" "My nose is too big and my arms and legs are huge!" "I hate myself!"

Well, every time she said these negative things about herself, the ole devil would smile. Can't you just image that by now he was grinning from ear to ear? But every time she would say one more bad thing about herself, God became sad and the angels would cry.

She decided that since she wasn't happy with her appearance, she was going to do something about it. So she took off walking down the trail that led to "Perfectville." It was a long, scary journey and she forgot to talk to God along the way and soon she became weary and lost.

She became very thin and she became very sick and she lost all of her strong muscles, but God never gave up on her. He would help her to get well. He would help her to find the way home.

So with the help of God, doctors, family and friends, she realized that on this earth, there is no such place as "Perfectville." She realized that God had created her in His own image, and that He loved her just the way He made her.

She asked God to forgive her and she asked God to heal her and to make her strong again so that she could tell other people about His wonderful power, love and grace.

God heard her prayers and He forgave her. He healed her and made her strong again. And she made a promise that she would NEVER AGAIN GIVE THE DEVIL ANYTHING TO SMILE ABOUT!!!!!

A good friend of mine once told me that every time we say or think something negative about ourselves, we make the devil smile. I had never really thought about it that way. In fact, I had never really given much thought to the devil, other than some people portray him as the little red man with horns, a pointed tail and a pitchfork, and some kids dress up as him on Halloween.

Oh, I know there is a devil and that he used to be one of God's angels. As an angel, his name was Lucifer, but he fell from the glory of Heaven when he wanted to overpower God. (Isaiah 14: 12-15) He then became Satan and one-third of the angels were cast out of Heaven with him and they became demons. (Revelation 12: 49) The Bible tells us that Satan is a liar; the father of all lies and he will deceive man in any way he can. (John 8:44) It also says in the Bible that Satan has become the "god of this world." (2 Corinthians 4:4) Because of this, Satan hates Christians and will try everything in his power to destroy our lives and our minds. (12)

I also know that when we say or think negative thoughts about ourselves, it makes God sad. God doesn't want us to find fault in ourselves because He says that we are all beautifully made in His own image. (Genesis 1:27)

I have always thought that it was just human nature to criticize ourselves, to not like certain parts of our body, to wish that we could look like someone else. Now, I am convinced that the devil and his demons play a huge role in the negative thoughts that come into our minds.

Whether it be in the form of an eating disorder or depression; whether it be suicidal thoughts or an addiction to drugs and alcohol, the devil is right there whispering in our ear, trying to make us believe things that aren't true. He whispers to us when we are weak, he prowls around like a lion trying to destroy us. He whispers things like "You are worthless, you are ugly, you are fat, you are stupid, nobody loves you. If you die, no one will care! If you eat that, you will be a fat pig! Just look at yourself in the mirror, you are disgusting!" And as he whispers, we get weaker, and as he lies to us, we start to believe his lies. Until one day, we vanish from ourselves and he controls our lives, and this is how the devil enters our minds. This is how he entered Katelyn's mind. This is how the devil whispers in our ears. However, this isn't the end; the devil doesn't have the final word. Just because he is very much alive and well today, living on planet Earth, this doesn't mean that we cannot beat his games. What I'm trying to say is that in order to resist the temptations of the devil, in order to block out the whispers in our ear, we have to fully rely on God to give us the strength and the power that we need to banish the devil and his demons. This reminds me of a little child who doesn't want to hear what his brother or sister is saying, so he sticks his fingers in his ears and shouts "I can't hear you! I can't hear you!" That's what we have to do with help from God and prayers. We have to put our fingers in our ears and shout as loud as we can when the devil tries to place bad thoughts in our mind. "I can't hear you! I'm not listening!"

The devil knows that God is much more powerful, but he wants to see if we know that. We must denounce the devil in our homes and from our family and children. We must rebuke Satan, in the name of Jesus Christ, who has shed his blood for our sins, and whose blood covers us and protects us.

Now, I'm not an expert on eating disorders, addictions or depression, and I'm not trying to say that if you suffer from one of these conditions that you should stop seeing your doctor or taking your medication. I'm not saying that all you have to do is stick your fingers in your ears. No, what I'm saying is that God will help you to know which doctor to go to and which medication is right for you, just like God revealed to us through research which type of treatment was right for Katelyn, the Family Based Maudsley Treatment.

If you trust God and believe without a shadow of a doubt that He will help you, if you banish the devil to the ends of the earth, if you believe in the almighty power of prayer, then God will stop the voices in your head and He will silence the whispers in your ear.

October 31, 2010

Good News: Katelyn came home from her grandmother's house and she was jumping up and down. "I ate some candy, I ate some candy!" Are you proud of me, Mom? Are you proud of me?" Then she danced around the house, "I ate candy! I ate candy!" I hug her "Yes, I am proud of you!" but in the back of my mind I know that the "high" feeling will go away soon! I know the reality will set in soon! The tears will start, the voices in her head will start, the doubts will start, the sit-ups in her room in the middle of the night will start, and the jogging in the shower will start! When will we see the end?

November 4, 2010

The evil demon reared his ugly head again today! Katelyn had a meltdown about having to drink the Carnation Instant mix with her milk at night. The dietician said this would help to add more calories to her daily intake. The word "calorie" doesn't set well with Katelyn. She curled up in a ball on the couch and cried. "I don't understand. Why do I have to drink it?" I want to scream! What do you NOT understand about dying!!! If you don't gain weight, you could die! I am not in the mood to argue with her tonight!

I told her that when she was a little girl, she understood perfectly that if she played in the street,

65

she could get hit by a car and die. So, why can't she understand that if she doesn't eat and gain weight, she could die?

Trent loses his patience, she cries even more. Landee just goes to bed early and I storm out of the room without telling anyone goodnight. Maybe when I wake up in the morning, this nightmare will be over!

December 6, 2010

It's 10:23 P.M. -Katelyn comes running into my bedroom. "Mom, you'll never guess what just happened!" One of the girls who has been so mean has just texted her and asked for forgiveness. The girl said, "I have been a terrible friend and I'm sorry. I know that the devil made me act like that." Katelyn tells her that she forgives her! Thank you, Lord, for little miracles.

March 21, 2011

Katelyn has regained all of her weight back, but because her metabolism is so messed up, she continues to gain more weight than she wants to. She's getting depressed again because all of her clothes are now too tight. She's beginning to exercise excessively again and doing sit ups in her room. She's beginning to skip meals again trying to lose some weight. We have an appointment with the dietician this week, maybe she can help. I have the feeling that everyone at school will be talking about her again because of the weight she is gaining. When will the demons in her mind leave? Only when God says it's time.

March 23, 2011

A boy came up to Katelyn today at school and said that he was sorry for how mean he had been to her all year. I'm so proud of Katelyn. She looked at him straight in the eye and replied, "It's the devil who makes people act mean to other people who are in need or during trials in their life. I forgive you!"

"The Lord is close to the broken hearted and saves those who are crushed in spirit." Psalm 34:18 NIV

8. HER TENDER HEART WAS BROKEN

It's now late August, it's 2:00A.M. and I can't sleep as usual. I hear crying coming from Katelyn's room, so I tiptoe down the hall to find out the reason for the tears. Her room has been filled with a lot of tears lately.

She is sitting on the floor, in her dark room, with her knees tucked into her chest. She is rocking back and forth and through her sobs, she says in a voice that I don't recognize, almost in a chanting manner… "I'm a good girl, I'm a smart girl, I'm a good girl" and then without skipping a beat, she changes the tune of the chant to a hiss through clenched teeth… "I'm worthless, nobody likes me, they hate me, I hate myself." This goes on for several minutes and she doesn't even realize that I'm in her room.

I sit on the floor beside her and wrap my arms around her. I want to protect her from the voices. I try to snap her out of this trance. She is crying so desperately that it takes a while to calm her down. Then through sobs, she confides in me that some bad things have happened today. Mean things have been said by people that she thought were her friends. They told her that no one likes her and that everyone is tired of her getting so much attention because of her illness. They're tired of people asking them about her. They told her they don't care if she's sick. They call her a liar.

Her tender heart is literally broken by these harsh words coming from people she once trusted. As we sit in the dark and I try to comfort her, I look around her room and see all the memories and pictures of these past friends. My heart is broken too!

She looks at me with terror in her eyes and tells me that her heart hurts. "I know sweetie", I say, "My heart hurts too." Then she grabs at her heart slowing pounding in her chest and whispers "I think I'm having a heart attack!" Our family doctor has told us that with low weight and low heart rate, a heart attack could occur, even though just a few weeks earlier an EKG had determined that her heart is healthy. She has already lost muscle tone and she has started to drag one leg. I'm not a medical expert, but I know that the heart is a muscle too and that this could be serious.

I leave her for just a second as I run to our bedroom and wake Trent. He reaches for the phone and calls his mother, who lives just down the road, to come to our house and stay with Landee. We don't wake her. We don't want her to worry. She has a volleyball tournament in the morning and she needs her sleep. She needs to have a normal life like her friends.

I wrap Katelyn in her favorite blanket, the blanket that she's had since she was a baby, and Trent carries her tiny body to the car. Even though it's August in Texas, Katelyn is freezing, her body temperature is low. As we speed the three miles to the hospital, Katelyn keeps asking me if she's going to die. She tells her Dad, "Please hurry because I'm dying!"

She tells me that she's sorry for being sick and she asks me if it's her fault. She asks me to tell Tanner and Landee "goodbye" and to tell them that they have been the best brother and sister that anyone could have, and she's sorry that she hasn't been a better sister.

She asks me if God will forgive her. She asks me if God will think that she did this on purpose. She wants to know if God still loves her. As Trent drives and I hold my sweet girl in my lap, wrapped in her baby blanket, I say, "Yes, God loves you and we love you, and we are not going to let you die" and I say a silent pray that God will heal our daughter.

The emergency room doors at the hospital open automatically and Trent carries Katelyn inside. She is gasping for air and whispering for someone to help her. The nurses motion us to lay her on the nearby examining table. The table is cold and Katelyn shivers. The nurses want me to fill out the necessary paper work. I hand them our insurance card. I am not leaving her side! As the doctor-on-call examines Katelyn, we tell him about her anorexic condition and that we think she may be having a heart attack. We inform him of the night's events, which have led to her broken heart.

He frowns at her boney body and immediately orders tests, an EKG and a chest x-ray. By now Katelyn is breathing easier, the pain has subsided and she has calmed down. A kind nurse that we have never met before holds her hand and tells her that she is a beautiful, precious girl.

It seems like an eternity before we hear the results, but the reports come back normal, she is not having a heart attack. In fact, the doctor informs us, in spite of her low weight, she is very healthy. Her heart rate is good and the chest x-ray revealed that her heart is in good condition. Her blood pressure is good and her internal organs are functioning properly. Her electrolytes and potassium levels are normal. Then he proceeds to diagnose a "panic/anxiety attack" which can sometimes feel like a heart attack. Or could it be "broken heart syndrome?" The Mayo Clinic released a report that "broken heart syndrome" is a temporary heart condition brought on by stress. People experiencing this may have sudden chest pains and think they are having a heart attack. (13) I say another silent prayer of thanks that her heart is healthy.

By now it's 5:00 A.M., and we leave the hospital, thankful that our daughter is alive and exhausted by the experience. Trent drives us home and carries Katelyn to her bed. The doctor has given her a mild sedative and tells us she will probably sleep for hours. I lay on the floor beside her bed and wait for the dawn. I listen to her soft breathing, but I don't sleep. I look at the ceiling and replay the night's events in my mind. My thoughts are whirling in my head...*My seventeen year-old daughter is sick and I hurt! I want the world to stop and hurt too! I want people to care! I want people to feel what we feel! I want people to be nice! I want friends to reach out to her! Is that so much to ask?*
- from my journal August 2010

Months after this traumatic incident, Trent and I discovered that without even knowing it, we both had surrendered Katelyn's life to God that night. At different times during that night, we had both fallen to our knees in prayer and told God that if He was ready for Katelyn to be in Heaven with Him, then we were willing to let her go. As much as we love her, we know that God loves her a million times more. He created her, and He only entrusted her to us for a short time. As much as we would miss her and her beautiful smile, with the one dimple in her left cheek, we had not seen that smile for a while, and we knew that she would be in Heaven with God. She would be happy and safe. She would never again be tormented by the devil's voice in her mind.

God heard our prayers that night, as we were on our humbled knees, and He knew our hearts were sincere. When God saw that we were totally willing to give our daughter to Him with complete faith and trust, He gave her back to us wrapped in His protective arms. Katelyn's story wasn't ending that August night in the hospital emergency room. Her story was just beginning so that we could share God's power and love with the world.

I shared this story with someone recently who I have known for many years, and I thought would understand. As I finished telling the story, I received a blank stare. This person had no idea what I was talking about. I then referred to the Bible, in Genesis, when Abraham was willing to sacrifice his son Isaac and when God saw that he was willing to let Isaac go, God gave him back to Abraham. I continued by saying that Katelyn isn't ours, she was given to us by God for only a short time, for us to raise and care for, and at any time, God can take her home with Him, and we have to be willing to let her go. "God gives, God takes. God's name be ever blessed." (Job 1:21 MSG) The response I got from this was "I can't believe you gave Katelyn permission to die!"

I didn't give Katelyn permission to die, but I did turn her life completely over to God. Before Katelyn's illness, I was literally scared to death of death. My biggest fear in life was that one of my children would die before I did. Now I realize that my children are not my children, they are God's children and a gift to us. "Don't you see that children are God's best gift?" (Psalm 127:3 MSG) and God can take them home at any time, and they will live forever in Heaven with their Heavenly Father! Because we are Christians, death is not bad! Death is not the end!

December 6, 2010

Katelyn is in a good mood today, and she is eating so well. One of her friends has written an English essay about her; how she is an inspiration because of what she is going through and yet she keeps on going with a positive attitude. On calm days like this, I think back to this summer when we were in the midst of all this with no hope for the future. Or at least I couldn't see the hope and I wasn't putting my faith in God.

I remember the middle of the night in August, when Katelyn sat on the floor in her room rocking back and forth and saying over and over again "I'm a good girl, I'm a good girl, I'm a smart girl, I'm a smart girl." I tried to hold her, but I don't think it was Katelyn in that body.

I think about this past summer when she started dragging her leg as she walked because she had lost all muscle tone. I think about when we spent the night in Lubbock at Tanner's house and she was so cold. We couldn't get her warm even with a sweat shirt, two pairs of sweat pants and three blankets and it was in the middle of the summer.

I think about how far we have come and I think

about how far we have to go.

March 13, 2011

I read this in a book today...“You have to die to yourself in order to live for Christ!” (14)

Every time Katelyn was hurt by one of her friends or hurt by words and rumors at school, she died a little inside. Every time we were hurt by seeing her hurt, we died a little inside. Every time we were hurt by our friends or family who didn't support us or who talked about us...we died a little inside. It felt like our hearts were literally breaking, but we have to die to ourselves before we can live for Christ.

"A friend loves at all times…" Proverbs 17:17

9. FINDING THE SONG IN HER HEART

In a novelty store one day, I saw this saying on a plaque, "A friend is someone who knows the song in your heart…And can sing it back to you when you have forgotten the words!"(15) When Katelyn was sick with anorexia, she forgot the words to the song in her heart. She lost the sparkle in her eyes as they sank into her thin face with no emotions. She lost her bubbly personality, she became withdrawn, she became depressed, and she became possessed with the evil demon known as an eating disorder that controlled her mind. As sad as it may be, many of her lifelong friends gave up on her and didn't try to help her find her song.

Many people have asked me, "why would close friends turn their backs on someone who was going through such a difficult time in their life? That's when friends are needed the most." I honestly don't have an answer. Maybe they didn't understand this illness, maybe they were scared for Katelyn's life, maybe they were mad at her because they thought she could control the illness, maybe they were jealous of all the talk around school, or maybe the devil was also whispering in their ear.

Whatever the reason, Katelyn was deeply hurt that these friends had forsaken her. One day she told me, "I really want to get well, but how can I get better when I have to go to school every day and face the people who have hurt me so much?" We began to see a pattern of sadness during the school week and then a little glimpse of sunshine during the weekends and then a dark gloom when Monday mornings rolled around. Every day at school she was tormented by their actions and every day she would come home from school crying. Some may ask why we didn't just take her out of school and home-school her. We seriously thought about it, we researched it and we talked to the school counselor and then we let Katelyn make the final decision. She told us that she wanted to try and live a normal life and she was a senior who had worked so hard to keep her grades up. She wanted to wear a cap and gown and walk across the stage with the other graduates. She didn't want to miss out on all the senior activities because you are only a high school senior once, and she realized that maybe God had some really big plans for her and He was teaching her perseverance.

God must have some really big plans for her because she received hateful phone calls and text messages. She was ignored, shunned, excluded from conversations and activities. She was whispered about and pointed at. Some drew pictures of her as a skeleton and made fun of her baggy clothes. I was told about the skeleton picture by a person who actually witnessed it. As the story was related to me, chills ran down my spine as I envisioned the three culprits sitting at their desks, scribbling and giggling about their creative portrait. When they grew tired of this amusement, they stabbed the drawing with a pencil, crumbled it up, and threw it in the trash. This was their way of saying that they didn't care whether Katelyn lived or died. They started rumors about her, gossiped about her, talked about her behind her back, and some were even bold enough to make fun of her to her face. Katelyn tried to be nice to them in return, but this usually was met with a cold shoulder and the "rolling of the eyes." If we would ask Katelyn how she was able to tolerate such mean behavior, she would tell us that she knew the devil played a big part in their actions and that she would pray for them. These actions weren't just revealed to us by Katelyn. In a way, maybe that would have been less painful. We were informed almost every day by other students at school who witnessed how Katelyn was being treated. One person was even shunned by the group because she was seen being nice to Katelyn. Teachers told us what they saw, it broke their hearts and some tried to intervene. Other parents called us when their children came home from school upset about the treatment of Katelyn. Every time I heard one more incident of meanness, I cringed inside. I had engraved one statistic of anorexia in my head: *"twenty percent of anorexics will die, of this number, half will be from suicide."*(6) Please, Lord, I begged, she can't survive the torment of this illness along with this cruelty. This disease has robbed her of her senior year; we can't let it rob her of her life!

It wasn't just her friends that turned away. Our family had some really close friends who turned away from us too. No phone calls, no words of encouragement, no prayers. This made me realize that Proverbs 17:17 pretty much sums it up, "A friend loves at all times...", during good times and bad times. So another one of my daily prayers became, "Dear Lord, please help us to forgive these people who have hurt us so much, and please, Lord, send us friends who will stay by our side and help us through this."

God did send some wonderful friends, who sang her song back and helped Katelyn to recover. I'm not going to

77

mention any names, but they know who they are and they will always be cherished in our hearts. These wonderful friends called, texted, and face-booked words of encouragement. They sent cards, Bible verses and left notes on Katelyn's car. They rejoiced with her accomplishments and cried with her disappointments, but most of all, they prayed for her, protected her and loved her in spite of this illness.

One thing that I have learned from this journey is that when a family is dealing with a terrible illness, such as cancer, the community will rally around that family with prayers, inspiration, food, and support for others in the household affected by the disease. When a family is dealing with a mental illness, most people don't know what to do or say, so they do nothing at all. I made a promise to God that I would never become one of the people who do nothing at all. Maybe we are all given just one chance to make a difference in someone's life. The people who chose to turn their backs on Katelyn, what if this was their one chance? When we all stand before God one day, will He say, "Well done my good and faithful servant?" (Matthew 25:21 NIV) "Whatever you did for one of the least of these brothers of mine, you did for me" (Matthew 25:40 NIV) or will God say "I never knew you. Away from me, you evildoers!" (Matthew 7:23 NIV)

As I look back on that year, I remember the words of an eating disorder counselor, who we had spoken to over the phone during the summer. She asked us if we knew what happened to a wounded chicken in a hen house. Trent grew up on a farm so he knew what she was talking about, but we didn't understand the relevance of the question to our situation. She proceeded to tell us that if there was a wounded chicken in a hen house, all the other healthy chickens would peck the wounded one to death. She used this illustration to prepare us for what would happen when Katelyn returned to school after the summer break and all the other kids realized that she was sick. As bad as it had been during the summer, and as much as we tried to protect her, when she went back to school, some of the other kids would "peck her to death." I didn't want to believe this. I just knew in my heart that all of Katelyn's friends would reach out to her and try to help her. She had lots of friends, she was nice and well liked, she was popular, but when school started in August 2010, the "pecking" began.

October 25, 2010

It's so hard to send Katelyn to school knowing what she has to face each day! She has faced being made fun of, being talked about behind her back, being talked about right to her face. I want to pinch their heads off! I want to ask them "What is wrong with you? Why are you so mean?" I asked Katelyn what we should do. What does she want me to do to protect her? She said to do nothing. She begged me not to say anything or make a big scene. She said all this is making her stronger. All this will make her a better person. She said that God wants her to pray for them. If she says something mean to them, then she is acting just like them. Two friends call me and said that this is "bullying." They said that we need to take a stand. They said that Katelyn's emotional state is too weak to take this kind of treatment. I pray every day for God to help me to know what to do and to help me to know what is the right thing to do for my precious daughter. I ask God to reveal to me what He would do. If this hurts me so much, then it must hurt Him a thousand times more. He watched His own son being persecuted. He knows the pain I feel. I pray that the answer will come to me! I pray that Katelyn can make it through one more day! I pray that Katelyn will learn how to stand up for herself in a Christian manner.

November 19, 2010

Months ago when Katelyn was traveling by bus to an out of town football game, I put a Bible verse in her sack lunch to help her to make it through the trip. She kept the Bible verse and put it on the back of her car sun-visor. Yesterday, when more drama had happened at school, as she was driving with tears streaming down her face, that Bible verse on the little sticky note, flew onto her lap. She had even forgotten it was in her car. The Bible verse was: "If God is for us, who can be against us?" (Romans 8:31 NIV)

December 3, 2010

Isn't it weird that you can be best friends with someone for many years and then when you are going through a really rough time, they turn their back on you? We tell our kids to always try to be "the better person" in all situations, but after today, I told Katelyn that she tried to be the better person and it didn't work, so that is all God expects her to do. God doesn't want her to be a doormat! Trent always says "You can't reason with a skunk because no matter how hard you try, you will just end up smelling like the skunk!"

January 5, 2011

Katelyn and I took a walk today. She is able to do a little more exercise now. As we walked, she asked me, "Mom, did I act like that before I got sick? Did I act mean like they treat me? Last year, if I had a friend who had anorexia or going through a hard time in their life, would I have been there for them, or would I act like they are acting?" She thought for a minute and then answered herself, "No, I think I would have supported my friend!"

February 17, 2011

I talked with our pastor today about all the things that are happening at school and he agreed with me that God is preparing Katelyn for things that are going to happen in the future. He made a point that I haven't thought about. He said that by Katelyn wanting to be a teacher, God is preparing her to be able to work with parents who may not think that she is doing a good job or parents who complain. Also, God is giving her compassion to help children who have been abused or who are being made fun of by others. We know that God has a special plan for Katelyn and everything that she is going through will make her stronger and prepare her for tough situations in life.

"Do not be afraid or discouraged because of the vast army. For the battle is not yours, but God's." 2 Chronicles 20:15 NIV

10. THE ROLLER COASTER RIDE

Imagine for a minute that you are on a roller coaster ride. At first you tell yourself that you're okay and you reassure yourself that the ride will be over soon. The longer the ride goes on, with no stopping in sight, you begin to desperately want off. You might even begin to yell at the control guy to "please stop this ride and let me off now!" However, it doesn't seem as if the control guy is listening. The longer the ride goes on and on and on, you begin to get tired, aggravated, irritated and scared. Your courteous pleas for help soon become desperate cries of despair.

I have never much liked roller coasters, but as a kid, I rode them just to fit in with the other kids. As I got older, I couldn't take the constant ups and downs, twists and turns, especially the rides that go forward for a while and then go backwards. To be stuck on a roller coaster that never ends would be a nightmare, but I have just described what living with an anorexic is like. You and your whole family are on an emotionally roller coaster that never ends.

When Katelyn first become sick, we didn't know what to expect, and yes, we were scared. We had never dealt with anything like this before, but in college, thirty years ago, I had written a paper about eating disorders. How ironic that the study and research I had done for that paper would suddenly come flooding back into my memory. Okay, I said to myself, how hard can this be? My daughter is sick; she has a mental issue with food. She needs a doctor and she needs lots of love and support from her family. And so began our roller coaster ride.

During the course of her illness, some days were calm. Oh how I cherished those days. I can't ever thank God enough for those calm days. Like the day in January when Katelyn seemed to be doing so well with the eating program. Her mood swings were better and her depression seemed to be diminishing. It was on that beautiful afternoon that just the two of us decided to take a walk. As we strolled down a quiet, country road, the conversation was light, finally turning to the subject of college. For eighteen years we had planned, dreamed, and saved for college and that day was approaching fast. I didn't want to spoil the beauty of the day by sharing my fears, but these thoughts raced through my mind: Would she ever be able to go to college? Would she ever live a normal life? Could she handle living in the dorms? Would she ever meet new friends? On days like this, the answer to these questions would have been "yes," but as we gently glided forward on our everyday ride, we knew not to get too comfortable because at any given moment, we could find ourselves going backward.

This brings to mind the day in December when the roller coaster ride almost broke my spirit. We were six months into the eating disorder and Katelyn had been invited to a Christmas party. There would be food, lots of food, but surprisingly, she assured us that she wanted to go. There were no panic attacks, no tears, no begging to stay home, she was confident in her decision to go. I was so proud of her, as I said to myself "one step forward." Trent and I were enjoying a peaceful night at home when my cell phone rang. When I answered it, all I heard were uncontrollable sobs coming from what sounded like a dungeon. I knew it was Katelyn, but I couldn't understand what she was trying to tell me. Had she been hurt? Had she been in a wreck? Had something been said that hurt her feelings? I finally calmed her down enough to ask what was wrong. Through sobs, she explained that at the party, the food had looked and tasted so good, and she had eaten way too much. She was now lying on the bathroom floor, in her friend's home, because she felt miserable and wanted to throw up. While all her friends stood outside the door, asking if she were okay, she pleadingly whispered for me to help her. Oh no, the rumors at school had finally begun to subside, what would be the rumors now?

My heart sank into my chest because up until this point, she had never wanted to throw her food up. I knew the consequences if she started this pattern and I knew that we would have a whole new set of problems if she started binging and purging. I was angry, as I thought to myself, forget the one step forward, we are going five steps backwards. I managed to sound calm as I told her to get up off the floor, to tell her friends that she had an upset stomach and to come home immediately. As I hung up the phone, I glared at Trent and hoarsely said through clinched teeth, "I'm leaving! I can't handle this anymore! You deal with her! You better learn how to fill out scholarship and college applications because I won't be here, I'm done!" The look in his eyes was of sheer helplessness as I gathered my purse and searched for my keys. As I opened the back door to leave, Katelyn's car drove into the driveway. She flung open her car door, ran into my arms, and when I saw her tear stained face and her defeated slumped shoulders, I knew I wasn't going anywhere. She needed me and as I had done a hundred times before, I held her, reassured her and tried to quiet the voices in her head.

This roller coaster ride was making us all sick. How much longer could we stay on--a week, a month, a year? "Dear Lord," I prayed, "please help us to take one day at a time!" Only God would know that our roller coaster ride would last a whole year. If we could have foreseen the future, would we have been able to endure? I think that's why God doesn't want us to see the future. He just wants us to trust Him. If you asked me to get on that ride again, I can honestly say that with the help of God, I would do it all again if it meant helping my daughter to get well.

December 22, 2010

Dear God, when will this nightmare end? Katelyn went to a Christmas party tonight. Her supportive friends were there. She called crying from the bathroom of her friend's house. She said that she ate too much and that she felt like throwing up. She didn't know what to do. Everyone at the party knew she was in the bathroom, probably throwing up. I asked her if she could drive? She said "yes." She came home crying and said that she ate so much, but she just couldn't stop. She promised that she didn't want to throw up on purpose. She asked me what was wrong with her. Why can't she control herself? She told me she can't even be a normal teenager and go to a Christmas party. She's worried that now these friends will start more rumors about her at school.

I was so mad, I couldn't even say anything! I knew if I open my mouth, it wouldn't be helpful words, but hurtful words! I couldn't help her right now. I'm so tired of all of this! Landee came into the room and wanted to know what's wrong with Katelyn. Poor kid, she has to go through all of this too! It isn't fair to her! It isn't fair to any of us! I told Trent what I had been thinking all day-that if Katelyn starts making herself throw up, then I'm leaving! I don't know where I'm going or what I'll do, but I can't take this anymore! I told Trent I hope he is prepared to do all the scholarship and college stuff because I won't be here. He just stared at me, and then he asked me if I'm okay? That's all he knows to say-NO, I'M NOT OKAY!!! I'm living in a nightmare and then I have to spend Christmas with people that just don't understand or care! After Katelyn went to bed, I heard her crying. Long after midnight, Elizabeth, our dietician, texted me and told me that Katelyn had texted her, begging for help!

"Now faith is being sure of what we hope for and certain of what we do not see." Hebrews 11:1 NIV

11. ANGEL OF HOPE

"I believe there are angels among us, sent down to us from somewhere up above. They come to you and me in our darkest hours, to show us how to live, to teach us how to give, to guide us with the light of love." (15)

I truly believe that there are angels among us, whether it be a kind gesture from a friend or an act of random kindness from a stranger. Our "angel of hope" came to us in the form of a Medical Nutrition Therapist named Elizabeth Bay, Katelyn's dietician.

The counselor that we had been seeing all summer recommended that we find a dietician. Someone who could guide us through the nutritional values and calorie intake that Katelyn would need to gain weight. I was given two telephone numbers of dieticians in a town an hour away from where we live. After making the phone calls, I learned that one of them had recently moved to another city, and the other one was new and didn't have all the credentials that she needed at the time. So it would be at least six weeks before we could see her. We needed someone now!

I then contacted one of our local 4-H agents who specializes in Nutrition and Home Economics and asked her if she could recommend a dietician, but the only one she knew had recently moved also. So, I asked if maybe she could counsel Katelyn in nutritional values, but she didn't feel that she was qualified for that task.

I felt like I had hit a brick wall, but I didn't give up. I turned to God. A few days later, our family doctor called to let me know that a dietician, who lived two and half hours away, would be traveling to our town one day a week. He wanted to know if we would like to set up an appointment to meet with her. Thank you, Lord, for another answered prayer.

Because we needed to see a dietician on a weekly basis, we arranged with Katelyn's school to allow her to have a free period after lunch, so that she would have an extra-long lunch break. This way we could schedule all our appointments with the dietician during Katelyn's lunch break, and she wouldn't have to miss so much school. We were also trying to keep her as stress free as possible because the more school she missed, the more stressed she would get about her grades.

Our appointments were every week at the local hospital and during our first visit, Katelyn sat in my lap and cried. As Mrs. Bay informed us up front, direct and detailed about what needed to be done to help Katelyn gain weight, Katelyn, still sitting in my lap, looked at me and softly cried "Mommy, this is going to be so hard!" This was coming from a seventeen year old who hadn't called me "mommy" since she was two years old. It was another example of the control that this disease has over one's mind.

She informed us that she wasn't specialized to work with eating disorders, but she was the only dietician within one hundred and fifty miles. She cared about us and she told us that if we all worked together as a team, she knew that Katelyn would make a complete recovery. It wouldn't happen overnight or in a week or in a month, but someday, we would see the light at the end of the tunnel.

Before this first visit I didn't know what Katelyn's future might hold. I didn't know if she would be able to finish high school; I didn't know if she would be able to go to college; I didn't know if she would live a normal life; I didn't know if she would live to see tomorrow. She gave us our first glimpse of hope that Katelyn would recover, and as we continued to see her every week for a whole year, she became more than just Katelyn's dietician, she became our life-long friend.

As she counseled us, she also shared with us the story of her only child, Nolan, who was also seventeen and also a senior in high school. He had recently been diagnosed with "hemophilia", a disease in which the blood fails to clot normally, causing prolonged bleeding even from minor cuts. He was not allowed to do normal teenage activities such as sports or even ride a bike because of the possibility of an accident and bleeding to death.

Several of his friends had also turned against him because of the lack of understanding of this disease. The first time Katelyn and Nolan met, he looked past her protruding cheek bones, past her sunken eyes and said, "You have a beautiful smile." Katelyn made this comment about him once, "Isn't it strange how someone who just met me can be so supportive of me and this disease, but people that I've known all of my life, suddenly don't care?" They continued to encourage each other through the year, they both graduated with honors from different high schools, and they both attend universities. Today they both know the struggles they have faced have only made them stronger.

90

October 6, 2010

Katelyn and I went to see her dietician today. Katelyn really likes her. She has a son who is a senior too and he has an illness too, so we can relate to what she is going through. She gave me "hope" today! She said that it will take a long time, but Katelyn will be ready to go to college next Fall. We will wait patiently and pray!

October 14, 2010

We saw the dietician today. She says she is proud of the way that Katelyn is eating. We showed her the daily food journal. She's concerned though because she has heard rumors that Katelyn is throwing up at school. (She doesn't even live in this town and yet she hears the rumors of a small town). Katelyn immediately started crying. No, she doesn't throw up! We are sick of all the hurtful rumors!

I have never seen, heard or found any evidence that Katelyn is throwing food up. I know she used to want to throw up because she couldn't stand how the food felt in her body, but she says she doesn't and I have to believe her!

November 3, 2010

The dietician is pleased with Katelyn's progress, but she says in the near future we will have to increase Katelyn's calorie intake. I don't know how I am going to do this, but God knows and He will help me! She starts Katelyn on a glass of Carnation Instant Breakfast with whole milk at bedtime. I could see the look of panic on Katelyn's face! She is almost defiant. I guess that would be a normal reaction for a normal teenager, but she has never been defiant about anything, until this illness. On this subject, she has to agree with us that she needs more calories. The minute she walks in the door after school, she burst into tears. I am thinking, what now? She's just overwhelmed about having to increase her calories.

December 2, 2010

We had an appointment with the dietician today. We haven't seen her in two weeks because of the Thanksgiving holiday. She is pleased with the progress and weight gain. We had a very productive meeting until the very end and that's when she told Katelyn that her face is beginning to fill out and she patted Katelyn's stomach and said that her stomach was filling out too. I could see the panic in Katelyn's eyes, but she didn't say anything until we

92

got in the car, then she burst into tears. "I don't want the weight gain to go to my stomach! That is my biggest fear, that I will gain all the weight back and it will go to my stomach!" More hours of reassuring her that weight gain is good!!!

August 19, 2011

Today was our last visit with our dietician. Katelyn leaves for college this weekend and she has regained all her weight and reestablished normal eating habits. It's a happy day, but also a sad day. We have become so close to her over this past year. We have seen her every week since last August. Not only did she help Katelyn to get well, she became our close friend. I don't know if Katelyn would have made it through this if she didn't have the trust and special bond with Elizabeth.

"And we know that in all things God works for the good of those who love him, who have been called according to His purpose." Romans 8:28 NIV

12. PART OF GOD'S PLAN

"It is doubtful whether God can bless a man greatly until He has hurt him deeply." A.W. Tozer

My dad tells a story of when he was a little boy growing up during the Great Depression in the 1930's. He was the youngest child in a family of eight boys and his mother raised these eight boys by herself. His mother worked several jobs to put food on the table for these hungry kids and in her spare time, she made beautiful quilts to sell for extra money. My dad remembers being a young child about four or five years old and watching his mother diligently sewing on the quilts. I'm sure her back was aching, after working all day, as she bent over the quilt that was spread out on the quilting frame. My dad would crawl under the quilting frame and pretend that he was in a tent with the sides of the quilt hanging down. As he would lie there on his back and look up underneath the quilt, all he saw were threads hanging down and an unfinished pattern. He told his mother that he didn't think the quilt was very pretty. Knowing my Granny, she probably scolded him for being under there in the first place and then she would use this as an opportunity to tell him stories about God. Granny told him that when you look underneath the quilt, you can't see the finished work or the pretty patterns, but when you look at the top of the quilt, you can see its beauty. Then she explained that just like in our life, we sometimes don't understand why things happen and our life seems full of scattered pieces that don't make sense. When we turn our life over to God, He will put all the pieces together and make something beautiful, because God has a plan and everything that happens in our life is part of God's plan. We may never fully understand the reason for God's plan. I don't think God wants us to have all the answers. He wants us to trust Him and rest assured that everything works according to His purpose, but when I get to Heaven, I want to ask God to help me understand the purpose behind an incident that happened during the time of Katelyn's illness.

I will never forget that day, the day that we felt helpless to protect our children, the day that our parenting skills were questioned. I have been a mother for twenty-two years and as long as I can remember, all I have ever wanted to be is a mother. I have a Bachelor's degree in Business, but I gave up my career as an accountant to stay at home and raise our three children because that's what Trent and I thought was best for our family. I have devoted my entire life to our children and now I am being told that they may be taken away from us.

I felt like I had been stabbed in the heart, punched in the stomach, and slapped in the face all at the same time. I felt confusion, mistrust, anger, denial. I felt as if my home, my palace, had been invaded by the enemy and that I had been dethroned from my position as a mother and as a protector.

We all occupy honored positions in life given to us by God and my position of being a mother was being attacked.

Now it was my turn to say "I don't understand! I don't understand!" But I knew this was part of God's plan and I knew I had to wait patiently to see His plan unfold.

In the meantime, I searched for Biblical answers that would help me to understand and that would heal my wounded heart. One day, I heard Woodrow Kroll of "Back to the Bible" on the radio and it sounded like he was speaking directly to me. He said, "God loves you even when you are dethroned. When you have been dethroned, God is preparing you for a better throne."(17) Maybe God is preparing us to sit by His throne in Heaven because painful events help us to grow closer to God, and this was a very painful event.

That day, September 1, 2010, started out to be a normal day, as normal as our days had been during the last few months. Katelyn had a doctor's appointment early in the morning before her first class started and an appointment with the dietician during her lunch break. She was in a good mood, she had eaten a good breakfast and I had already packed her lunch that she would eat during the dietician's visit.

As I drove Katelyn to school after seeing the doctor that morning, my cell phone rang. I had turned it off while in the doctor's office and I noticed I had missed a call from an unknown number, but this call was from Trent, probably wanting to know about the doctor's report. I could sense from his shaky voice that something was wrong as he asked if Katelyn was still in the car. "Yes, she's right here, do you want to talk to her?," I replied.

"No," he whispered, "Just listen and stay calm. Don't let Katelyn know what I'm telling you! A caseworker tried to call you, I'm so glad he got me instead."

By now we were at the school and I drove up to the door to let Katelyn out. I tried to sound calm as I hugged her and said, "Bye, love you, have a good day, see you at the dietician's at 12:30." As she shut the car door, I took a deep breath and listened to what Trent had to tell me. What he said next would change our lives forever.

"We have been reported to the Child Protective Services for medical neglect and we're being investigated TODAY! We have to get statements from our doctor, the therapist, the dietician, and the coaches at school. We have to get Katelyn and Landee out of school early this afternoon for an interview with the CPS Caseworker. Are you still there? Did you hear what I just said?"

I was speechless. I was numb. I was in shock. Was this a joke? Was this a dream? The sound of a car honking behind me snapped me back into the harsh reality and then the first of millions of tears began to flow.

The rest of the morning was a blur as I rushed around trying to get the necessary documents needed to prove to the CPS Caseworker that we had never, nor would we ever, abuse or neglect our children. Up until today, I didn't know very much about the Child Protective Services other than what I had heard, that parents are basically "guilty until proven innocent" and that CPS has the power to remove children from their homes and place them into foster homes. I know that CPS is a program that was implemented to protect innocent, abused children and I'm thankful that there's such a program, I just never imagined my family would be involved in an investigation. Terrifying thoughts ran through my mind. What if they don't believe us? What

97

if we can't prove that we are getting Katelyn help? What if they take the girls away from us? Will Katelyn and Landee be scared? Would this added stress send Katelyn into a relapse? And then I realized that not once since the phone call from Trent had I prayed about the situation. So I pulled the car over to the side of the road and I prayed out loud asking God to comfort all of us, to keep us brave and to protect us.

Trent and Katelyn met me at the dietician's office for the scheduled appointment at noon. I wanted to get there first so I could tell the dietician the news and get a statement from her before we told Katelyn, but they were all there first, so, we began the session. I'm sure that by looking at my swollen eyes, everyone could tell that something was wrong. When the session was over and Katelyn was eating her sack lunch, we relayed the news and asked for the medical statement. At first Katelyn wasn't sure of what all of this meant, but as she watched her Dad choke back the tears as he tried to explain, she immediately knew that it must be something really bad. Then our sweet seventeen year old daughter climbed into my lap, buried her face in my chest and sobbed, "I'm sorry Mommy, I'm sorry."

We tried to explain to her that this was not her fault. She was sick and she didn't do anything wrong. This was one more step backward in the healing process of which we had taken so many steps forward.

By now, everyone in the room was crying, even Mrs. Bay, who didn't know us very well at this time. She works in the medical field, she knows the repercussions that a CPS investigation can have on a family and she felt our pain. Katelyn asked if she could just go home and not go back to school for the afternoon, she couldn't go to school and concentrate while she worried about the future of her family. The CPS investigation was this afternoon anyway, so Katelyn went home with Trent and I went to the school to get Landee. I found her in sports class practicing volleyball, and when she saw me, she immediately knew that something must be wrong because, first, she didn't know I was coming and second, the coaches really frown on taking athletes away from practice unless it's a family emergency. I told the coaches that I needed to take her home because, yes, it was indeed a family emergency. As we hurriedly walked to the car, Landee breathlessly asked, "Mom, what's wrong? Did someone die? Is Katelyn okay?" How do you easily tell your child that her parents have been accused of child abuse and neglect? By now, Landee was crying too.

When we arrived home, the CPS Caseworker was already inside talking with Trent and Katelyn. He was very nice and soft-spoken and we all sat around the dining room table as if we had invited him to Sunday dinner. He looked to see if the house was clean, if there was food in the pantry and then he explained the situation. Trent and I had been reported to CPS for medical neglect due to Katelyn's weight loss. The report stated that we "refuse to get Katelyn any medical treatment" and that's why he needed the medical statements from our doctors. Even though the investigation revolved around Katelyn's health, Landee was included also because she's a minor still living in our home. If it were deemed that we were "unfit parents," both girls would be removed from our care and placed with strangers. We were instructed to call Tanner and place him on "stand-by" since he was twenty-one and living at college, but his statement may be needed to support our parenting skills. The caseworker went on to explain that he would need to interview each of us, individually, while the others stayed in another room. He would need to video record the conversations and take pictures (which I refer to as mug-shots) of the girls. He told us that during the next few weeks, he would interview any doctor who had recently treated Katelyn and he would go to her school to interview the principal, the school counselor and the coaches. It would take a few weeks for the investigation to be concluded, and depending on the outcome, the girls could be placed in foster care. We were instructed to have small suitcases prepared with their favorite things, just in case. When Trent protectively asked how they could take our children away from us, the caseworker matter-of-factly stated, "By sheriff's force, if you resist."

Katelyn was the first to be interviewed, and we were instructed to go to separate rooms. Then it was Landee's turn. Our house isn't very big and the walls aren't very thick, so I could hear her crying as she answered questions. Next they interviewed Trent, and then me. I'm not sure what they were asked because afterward, we were too emotionally drained to talk, but one question that I remember being asked, really pierced my heart. I was asked, "Do you withhold food from Katelyn as a form of punishment?" Really, I thought!

After the caseworker left, we all just stared at each other in silence. It was a Wednesday and the girls always go to our church's youth Bible study on Wednesday nights, but none of us wanted to go anywhere. It was as if we were clinging to each other because we feared that we would soon be separated. Now came the time to make some phone calls. I needed to call Tanner, my parents and my sister. Trent needed to call his family. We desperately needed their support and their prayers. Everyone we spoke to had the same reaction, shock, especially Tanner. He wanted to come home right then. He was an adult now, he reasoned, he would take care of his sisters. No, he needed to stay in school. We are the parents. We will take care of our children. Besides, everyone who knows us knows that we are good parents and that we take care of our children. This must be the work of the devil. The devil hadn't been successful in taking Katelyn's life, so now he was focusing on the next best thing, taking her away from her home.

For three days after this incident, I sat in a dark room, in silence, and barely spoke to anyone. I went into a deep depression and I didn't eat or sleep. My home phone and my cell phone rang constantly, but I never answered them. For the next few weeks, Landee worried and cried herself to sleep each night. She would ask when we would know the final outcome of the investigation. Katelyn became withdrawn again because she felt guilty that this was happening to our family due to her health. Then one day in late September, we were notified that the charges against us for medical neglect had been "ruled out" because our doctors provided more than enough information to conclude that Katelyn was getting enormous medical care.

I wish I could say that this was the end of our nightmare. We found out that because we had been investigated for child abuse and neglect, the title "alleged perpetrator" of medical neglect would remain on our background-check for a long time. People in our small community had heard about the incident and had already begun gossiping. It seems even if you are proven innocent, people still portray you as guilty.

Even though my number one priority was to help Katelyn get well, I decided that I wasn't going to just sit by and let someone accuse me or my husband of doing something that we didn't do. I was going to find out every stitch of information that I could about the Child Protective Agency and about our case. I requested copies from Austin of everything in the CPS files and after waiting four months, I received the information I requested, except, of course, the names of the people who reported us. Their names are protected under the Texas Family Code confidentiality laws. I learned there were two reports made by two people, but the contents in the reports were so similar, they had obviously worked together. Everything in both reports was very detailed, from Katelyn's weight and height, to specific doctors who diagnosed her. The only problem was that everything in the report was completely wrong, all false accusations, even the names of the doctors were wrong. The report stated that "her hair is falling out and her internal organs are shutting down. Her parents are doing nothing to get her help; they are trying to handle it by themselves." None of this was true.

I was furious that a state agency could come into our home, basically ruin our lives and reputations and leave emotional scars on our girls, all based on assumptions; lacking factual structure. I was furious that people, who didn't know all the facts and were basing their information on assumptions and rumors, could lie to CPS. We honestly believe that because they didn't talk to us about the "Maudsley" program or they didn't understand it, they assumed we were doing nothing. We decided to hire a lawyer to find out about our rights as parents because we felt our parental rights had been violated.

What we learned was very educational but very disheartening. Basically, anyone for any reason can pick up the telephone, or go to a computer to report someone of child abuse or neglect without having factual foundation. According to the "Good Samaritan Laws" and the "Mandatory Reporting Laws,"(18) professionals such as teachers, nurses, doctors, daycare operators are required to make reports of suspected child abuse. They face criminal penalties for failure to report. Texas Family Code Sec. 261.101 keeps the names of the reporters confidential, (18) but Texas Family Code Sec 261.107 makes it a criminal offense if someone makes a false report to a State Agency. (18) Our lawyer informed us that based on the statements of our doctor, dietician and therapist, we had enough evidence to prove the accusations of medical neglect made against us were false. Our next option would be to take the case before a grand jury. If convicted, the people who made the report would be indicted and/or arrested and/or go to jail. The final decision rested in our hands. We had to ask ourselves, are we seeking revenge? Are we seeking justice? Are we wanting to make this an example to people who abuse the system? Or are we trying to make sure this never happens to other innocent families?

Our final conclusion was that we want to teach our children about forgiveness and not about revenge or getting even. We didn't want to have someone arrested and sent to jail. We know that "two wrongs don't make a right." Per our lawyer, a case like this has never happened in our town, this would be smeared all over the local newspaper. In 1 Corinthians, Chapter 6, Paul wrote a letter to the church in Corinth telling them how Christians should act. One of his lessons was concerning lawsuits against believers. "Is it possible that there is nobody among you wise enough to judge a dispute between believers? But, instead, one brother goes to law against another-and this in front of unbelievers! The very fact that you have lawsuits among you means you have been completely defeated already. Why not rather be wronged? Why not rather be cheated?"(1Corinthians 6:5-7NIV)

Somehow, in making the decision to drop the case, I felt that I had failed to protect my children from the evil of the world, but I know it was the right decision and I know in the end, God has the final judgment. However, little did I know when I first read 1 Corinthians, how close that verse would hit home. After we learned the names of the individuals who reported us to CPS, we knew that if we had continued to pursue the case, it would have literally torn our entire extended family apart. We are totally convinced that the devil used these two people to break a strong Christian family apart, and we weren't going to let that happen. As much as it hurt us and our children, as much as we felt betrayed and lied to, we decided that just as God "hates the sin, but not the sinner," we can also hate what happened, but we don't hate the people involved.

As time passed, the deep depression that I felt on the first day of the investigation, stayed with me for a year and a half, causing physical ailments, including insomnia, headaches, and weight loss. Until one day, with the help of God, I decided that I would not let this consume my life for one more minute. Based on the Serenity Prayer, "God, grant me the serenity to accept the things I cannot change..." (19) I had to accept that I can't change what happened and I can't change the hearts of the accusers or the rumors in town, but I can change the bitterness in my heart. This new found freedom gave me the ability to pray for the people who have hurt our family and to begin the healing process.

October 31, 2010

Trent took Katelyn and Landee "Trick-or-Treating" tonight. The girls wanted me to go so badly. I used to love to go, but all that has changed since the CPS report. I don't want to be around people. I am so hurt, I am so mad!!! How could anyone think that I am not taking care of my children? How could anyone think that I am neglecting my children?

I hate this feeling-I hate that I don't want to be around people anymore. I hate that I am letting the girls down by not going with them tonight. I hate that all of this has changed our lives. One day I will look back and see God's plan in all of this.

December 8, 2010

We got the report back from CPS today. All the information in the report is completely false. All the feelings came rushing back and I cried again as I read the words "neglect or abuse" of my children. How could anyone think that I could "neglect" my children? I especially cried when I read the statements made by Katelyn and Landee. I know how scared they were being interviewed, video recorded and having their pictures taken by a total stranger. I know how scared they were when they were told they might be taken away from us and put in Foster Homes.

How dare someone do that to my innocent children! They have done nothing wrong! It makes me furious that someone was so stupid that they didn't think about what this would do to my children! How dare someone think that they know more about my children's health and well-being than I do! I am SO furious I can barely write this! I know that I have to forgive someday, but right now, it is really hard! I pray for God to give me the strength to forgive.

February 9, 2011

It has been six months since the CPS investigation and when I finally think I am doing better, something triggers negative thoughts and I go back into a depression again! I have been crying all night and into the day and I tell myself that I am just feeling sorry for myself, but I can't seem to shake it! I know the Bible says that we have to forgive and I pray every day that God gives me the strength and

106

wisdom to do the right thing. I don't like feeling like this-I don't like being angry and sad and depressed. I don't like the feeling of hatred that I have in my heart, and I know that God doesn't want me to feel this way. Lord, help me; I am trying so hard to get over this! I know that it's part of God's plan-all of this-and I am trying to accept that and learn from this! I know there is a reason for everything and everything works for the good of those who love the Lord. But I hurt so deeply! Sometimes I feel so alone, but I know God is with me and I know God feels my pain and I know He will help me through this shadow!

July 13, 2011

It has been almost a year since the CPS case. I am still having a very hard time accepting that someone wanted to take my children away from me! I dwell on it every day, rehearsing the words that I want to say to those people. I am sad and I cry a lot. I am depressed and the girls are noticing it.

Trent is trying to be understanding. He prays for me and he tells me that God wants me to let it go and forgive. I am really trying because I don't like this hatred and bitterness that I feel in my heart. I teach young children Sunday School every Sunday and I teach them about forgiveness-I feel like I am being a hypocrite!

Trent tells me that we should feel honored that the devil feels so threatened by our family and by our

107

children that he tried to kill our daughter and he tried to take both girls away from us through the CPS. Trent says that the devil knows that God has some wonderful plans for our children and the devil is threatened by that!

"Love does not delight in evil but rejoices with the truth. It always protects, always trusts, always hopes, always perseveres." 1 Corinthians 13:6-7 NIV

13. A SISTER'S LOVE

One night in Landee's room, as I was telling her goodnight, I asked about her day. As we talked and focused on the good parts of the day, I casually mentioned that I'd been thinking about writing a book based on the past year. She got excited and asked if she could write a chapter in the book. She joked that she wanted it to be chapter twenty-one because that's her favorite number. In her chapter, she wanted to tell her side of the story about living with an anorexic sister. "Sure, that's a great idea" I said, "but you better start keeping notes or writing in a journal about things that have happened or you might forget." She looked at me, with tears in her eyes and said, "Mom, I will never forget!"

Landee had just started high school as a freshman when all this began, the same high school that Katelyn attended. It's hard enough being fourteen starting high school, learning your way around a new building, meeting new teachers, making new friends, starting sports and new activities. Now top that off with having an anorexic sister, who is a senior and who everyone in school, including teachers, is discussing. Everywhere she went, whether it was school, church, or family gatherings, she overheard comments about Katelyn, some being of shock, some being of concern, some being of support, but most being negative and mean. Landee has never been a troublemaker. She has never had problems with teachers or other students. She has always been a straight "A" student, well liked, happy and funny, but this disease had affected our whole family and she was an innocent bystander in the midst of this storm.

As her grades began to slip and she began to act up in class, I realized that she was deeply hurting for her sister and herself. She became depressed and angry and she wanted to punch the mean people at school. Instead of punching the mean people, she began to punch the walls in our house. This wasn't our sweet, youngest child who could always make everyone laugh.

She began having nightmares about the CPS investigation. She cried herself to sleep for months, afraid that someone would take her away from the safety of her home and from her parents. When Katelyn would have bad eating days, Landee would beg and plead "You have to eat; Katelyn, if you lose more weight, someone will take us away, and then you might die!"

"Dear God," I prayed, "How do I help her through the pain? How do I protect her from the hurt? She hasn't done anything to deserve this. Show me how to help her, give me the words to comfort her, help me to be the Godly mother that you want me to be."

The answer came to me one night while I was watching a television special about Elizabeth Smart, the fourteen year old girl, who had been kidnapped and held in captivity for nine months, living through terror and torture. Her mother was asked by the reporter, "How did Elizabeth ever overcome what she lived through? How is she able to live a normal life or to go on with her life, and begin to heal and forgive?" I will never forget what her mother said... "She took the lead from me. If I dwelt only on the past and the hurt and I only stressed how awful that time in her life had been, and how we should all feel pity and sorrow for what had happened, then Elizabeth would feel the same way. So I took the lead and only focused on the positive things, such as how blessed we are that she is home and alive. And what happened, as horrible as it was, is only a very small part of her life. The best part of her life is yet to come. She followed my lead to become the beautiful, young woman that she is today." (20)

So, my daily prayer became that I would be mature enough to "take the lead" and to focus on all the positive aspects in our lives and not dwell on the negative parts. Also, to not feel sorry for myself that our family was going through such a difficult time, and for Tanner, Katelyn and Landee to be able to see in me an example of healing and forgiveness.

I wish I could say this was easy. I'm a forty-nine year old, middle-aged mature woman. I have seen and experienced the harshness dealt in life, but nothing could have prepared me for the deep pain I felt for my children, the anger and bitterness that consumed me, the mistrust and betrayal of close friends and family, the intense fear that someone else can dictate the raising of my children and there is absolutely nothing I can do about it. How does a fourteen year old even begin to grasp all of these emotions? Only a fourteen year old who has lived through it can answer that question, but I can tell you what I observed, what she could have done, and what she chose to do. She could have turned to alcohol, drugs or sex to numb the pain; she could have become rebellious; she could have spent years in therapy dealing with the hurt. She knew in her heart that bitterness, anger and hatred aren't how God wants us to live, so she turned everything over to God. She asked Him for forgiveness, and then, as the Bible says, "Repent and be baptized..." (Acts 2: 38), Landee, who was baptized as an infant, made the decision on her own to be baptized again, in a small country church, at the age of sixteen.

November 3, 2010

Landee has started going with us to some of the counseling sessions with the dietician. Maybe this will help her too. She told me that I need to pay very close attention to Landee so that she won't feel like we are focusing all our attention on Katelyn. She said that Landee may one day do something drastic just to get our attention. This disease has drained our whole family. I pray to God to help me give all my attention to my kids and to be the mother that He wants me to be.

December 19, 2010

Landee confided in me that she has been feeling sad and depressed. This is very unusual for her because she used to be so carefree and happy. I pray that all of this, Katelyn's illness, the meanness at school, the gossip, her anger over the way people treat Katelyn, the CPS investigation, and the tension between our family will not have a lasting effect on her.

March 28, 2011

Landee received an award at the Optimist Club Banquet tonight. It was an award given by the high school basketball coaches for the enthusiasm that she shows while playing basketball. Thank you, Lord, for allowing a little joy and recognition to come into her life because this had been such a hard year for her.

"I can do all things through Christ, which strengtheneth me." Philippians 4:13 KJV

14. LANDEE'S STORY

That moment of impact when I realized that I am a witness of God. That moment of impact when emotions become locked inside of a fourteen year old girl's head and the power of silence overwhelms the gift of laughter. I don't like to talk about it; I don't like to think about it. If I were asked to live it again, my answer would be "No", but I wouldn't trade those memories for anything in the world. I have a story now; this is my story.

Most events I couldn't comprehend what was happening. I just saw my sister everyday as skin and bones. Something was wrong, I realized, but when you live with that for a while it becomes normal. I was scared for Katelyn. I was scared about what might happen the next day. I didn't know the medical reports that well, but I knew when I heard the cries, it wasn't good. I had my funeral speech that I was going to say at her funeral planned out.

I knew I was changing too, hearing the whispers at school when she would walk through the halls. "That girl looks like bones!" "Why is she so skinny?" I didn't like to hug Katelyn, that wasn't my sister. It was just temporary. I would sneak salt in Katelyn's food because I thought salt adds weight, I didn't know any better. I just wanted everything to end and I wanted to wake up from the nightmare. I felt angry, sad, ignored, confused, but I never wanted to show my emotions. I tried to stay strong for my parents, so I didn't cry in front of my Mom or Dad. I always waited until I was alone. I was never ashamed of Katelyn. I love her and I wanted to protect her. I don't blame her for my anger issues. I never wanted to blame her for anything.

I think about that day fairly often, the day of the CPS investigation. The questions I was asked still run through my mind. I felt like a criminal, getting my picture taken, with tears down my face. I asked the man, as he took my picture, "Do I smile?" I don't think anybody could smile through a time like that. The question that most astonished me was "Do your parents ever beat you?" Silence would probably be the best answer, but shocked was my emotions.

No, my parents never beat me, but how could I make him understand that? I was a criminal in my own loving house! The man said the questions were just between me and him, but I told three of my friends. It is not my favorite subject to discuss, I was scared. I remember my Mom getting me out of volleyball practice. She had sunglasses on; she never wears sunglasses in a building. I knew something was wrong, but Katelyn was getting better, I knew she was okay. My first thought was that my dog had died or one of my grandparents had died. I begged my Mom to tell me as we were walking to the car. Then my next thought was that they can't take Katelyn away from me! Then I was told they could take me too. I can't really explain in words how I felt, but those emotions will always be engraved in my mind.

I never questioned God, though, about why this was happening to us. I was always told that God places challenges in our lives for a reason. Something I learned from this experience was to look past the smile on a face. People may be smiling on the outside, but hurting on the inside. No one ever saw past my smile. People saw me as the class clown, always making jokes to cover up what was happening. If Katelyn had a bad day, my day would be bad too. I wish we didn't have so many bad days.

It has taken me awhile to write an ending to my chapter. How does somebody end something like this? Well, let me tell you, this is not the end, just simply the beginning. I'm not afraid to say I've changed, maybe for the better, maybe for the worse, but one thing I would like to end with is this:

A loving family sticks together through thick and thin; blood and sweat; tears and pain, but in the end, comes out like a blooming flower that just suffered through a thunderstorm, vibrant and full of life, with no signs of damage.

March 29, 2012:

(It's been two years since Katelyn's illness and while she's away at college, Landee posted this on her "Facebook" page)

Sometimes I creep your Facebook and see how happy you are. I see how beautiful you are and I think about those times...those times we laughed and those times we cried, but even though we may say some hurtful words, we both love each other and we faced all those challenges together. I will never forget every smile I saw on your face. I love you!

April 23, 2012

I took Landee to the doctor today. She has been complaining of stomach aches, loss of appetite and she is losing weight. She has been diagnosed with stomach ulcers brought on by worry and stress. We talk about what she is worried about and why she is stressed. She wants to know if she will be taken away from us because she is losing weight. She is worried that someone will report us to CPS again. I reassure her that we will protect her and take care of her, but I think she has lost trust. She shouldn't have ever gone through that the first time, how can I promise her it will never happen again? I don't tell her that my biggest fear in life is that for the next few years, until she is eighteen, we will constantly be looking over our shoulder, wondering what lies are being told about us and wondering who is an enemy disguised as a friend.

"There is a time for everything…a time to weep and a time to laugh." Ecclesiastes 3: 1 & 4 NIV

15. FINDING LAUGHTER AMONG THE TEARS

"Lord, Thank you for letting me laugh today, but never let me forget that I cried!" (Unknown author)

If you were a stranger and had seen our family out in public during this year, you probably would have thought we were a normal family. We went to church every Sunday, we went to sporting events, we went to restaurants (usually without Katelyn) and we always had a smile on our faces. We tried to be normal, we tried to live our life as normal as possible. We knew that our kids needed a normal life, but our life was anything but normal. Before we turned our life over to God, before "we let go" of the situation and "let God" take control, our life was filled with sadness, desperation, tears and pain.

I became depressed and I cried all the time because of the hurt that I saw Katelyn going through. It took every ounce of strength that I had to get out of bed every day and take care of my family, but I knew that they needed me.

I was afraid, I was confused, I was bitter, I felt lost. I began to take sleeping aids at night to help me sleep because at least when I was asleep, I could dream and forget about the real nightmare going on around me. In the twenty five years of our marriage, I have seen Trent cry only a few times at funerals, now it became a daily event.

He felt helpless, his hair began to fall out, and he didn't have the answers. He's the father, he's the head of the household, he's supposed to be able to fix anything and to make everything better, but he couldn't fix this illness.

Katelyn cried every day because of the torment this illness was putting on her mind and her body. She knew that she had to get better; she knew that she had to gain weight, she wanted to get well, but the devil was still there whispering those awful things in her ear. It didn't help matters that she was ridiculed and made fun of every day at school.

The success of Landee's day was measured by the success of Katelyn's day. Every day when I picked Landee up from school, her first words were "How was Katelyn's day? Did she have a good day? Did she eat good today? Were people cruel to her today?" Also, remember that Landee saw and heard things going on at school too. If Katelyn had a good day, then Landee had a good day. If not, then Landee withdrew and cried herself to sleep more nights than not.

And Tanner, three hours away at college, stopped coming home to visit. He couldn't bear the meals spent in frustration. He couldn't bear to hear the stories of cruelty that his sister faced at school. He couldn't bring himself to hug Katelyn because he couldn't bear to feel her bones. And so, he stayed away.

Even in the midst of darkness, God did send laughter into our lives. Some of this laughter came in the form of three little boys, our nephews, ages six, eight, and ten. Their innocence and their child-like faith gave us something else to focus on. To them, Katelyn was just Katelyn, a cousin who they loved. They didn't judge her, they didn't make fun of her, they didn't question "why." I don't think they even noticed her physical appearance. They love her because she makes it very obvious that she loves them just as much.

October 6, 2010

We laughed today at the dinner table. That is something we haven't done in a long time. We laughed as a family. We had barbeque "little smoky" weenies, they were made of turkey and usually Katelyn will eat turkey. Today she can't eat them. She pushes her plate back and begins to cry. Landee tenses up and waits for the explosion. Trent points at Katelyn's plate and says "EAT THEM!!!" Katelyn frowns and says "Don't point at my weenies!" We all look at each other and burst out laughing.

October 9, 2010

Today it's nice to have something else to focus on. I'm keeping my little nephews all weekend while their little brother is in the hospital. It's nice to hear their laughter. It's nice to have laughter back in the house. I hear Katelyn squeal with laughter as she chases them around the house. They don't question why she's so skinny, they don't judge her, they love her just the way she is. Just for a little while, the darkness is gone.

October 20, 2010:

Today is my birthday. Katelyn asks me if she can make me a birthday cake. She loves to cook, but she won't eat anything that she cooks. I tell her that the only way I will allow her to make me a cake is if she will eat some of it too. You can see the wheels turning in her head. She will search every cookbook until she finds a "healthy" cake if she has to eat a piece too. She makes me a birthday cake with no sugar, only sugar-free applesauce and oatmeal and whole wheat flour. She uses non-fat yogurt as the icing, with fresh blueberries on top. When it comes time to eat the cake, she takes the lid off and mold is growing all over the top! The yogurt icing has caused the cake to mold. We all have a good laugh and we throw the molded cake away.

March 24, 2011:

I was driving in the car today and I thought of something funny that Landee had said yesterday. And I started to laugh; in the car; by myself; out loud. And I laughed so hard (by myself) that tears came to my eyes and people in other cars probably thought I was crazy. And then I remembered a time not too long ago that I didn't think I would ever laugh again. And I thanked God for letting me laugh again. And I thanked God for giving me the joy of Landee and for giving her the unique humor that only God can give.

"We were filled with laughter and we sang for joy." Psalm 126:2 NLT

16. CELEBRATION OF LIFE

In November of 2010, Katelyn celebrated her 18th birthday. We knew the day she was born that this would be a special day, but we didn't know then that this birthday would become a "celebration of life." A few months earlier, she could have died and we didn't know if she would even be alive to see her next birthday. However, this day dawned bright and beautiful, she was alive and getting healthier every day. We rejoiced.

Weeks before her birthday, we began planning for the "celebration of life" party. She decided on an elegant luncheon with finger foods, crystal glasses, fancy decorations, table clothes and center pieces. She spent hours planning the menu, the invitations, the décor and the party favors, which consisted of framed Bible verses placed at each guest's place setting.

Now came time for the guest list. She didn't want to exclude anyone. She didn't want to hurt anyone's feelings, but she knew that she only wanted to invite people who had been supportive of her during her illness. She only wanted to invite special friends who had been there for her. She wanted to invite the friends who had called or sent a card or text message, and the friends who had emailed or face-booked her kind, encouraging words. She only wanted to invite friends who had stood up for her, who had hugged her and encouraged her at school, and who had said "I am here for you."

Months before this party, I began praying to God to please send Katelyn a friend. Some of her closest friends had abandoned her, so I prayed for just one friend who would love her and support her, and encourage her during this difficult time in her life. God not only answered that prayer, but He multiplied it by twenty, because when the guest list was finished, Katelyn had written down the names of twenty friends who had helped her through this dark valley.

The party was beautiful, elegant and a huge success. Only two people that were invited weren't there. Nolan, our dietician's son, sent her a bouquet of flowers. She had never received a beautiful bouquet of flowers. Everyone got excited when the florist brought the flowers to the door.

As I watched everyone laughing and having a good time, tears filled my eyes and I was so thankful that God had allowed us to celebrate this special 18th birthday with our daughter and her friends.

Over the buzz of the laughter and the many conversations going on at the same time, I clicked my glass and asked if I could have everyone's attention. I told myself that I wasn't going to cry, but as usual, I did cry, and with tears in my eyes and a tremble in my voice, I told everyone that it wasn't just a coincidence that they were here today. I explained how months earlier, I had prayed for God to send them into our lives. I thanked each one of them for being there for Katelyn on that day and all the other days that they had supported her. Then we all raised our glasses in a toast for this "celebration of life."

November 14, 2010

We had a great Sunday, going to church as a family, eating a wonderful meal with no stress. We were just enjoying a relaxing afternoon at home watching football on TV. Katelyn was busy planning her 18th birthday party. She deserves to do something special with everything that she has gone through. I pray that the rest of the week will go as smoothly as today.

November 22, 2010

Katelyn is so excited about her upcoming birthday party. It's so good to see some joy back into her life. As usual, some of her enemies, the ones that used to be her friends, try to hurt her more and ruin this day for her. They have heard about her party, so they decide to have a party of their own and broadcast it all over "Face Book." She doesn't seem bothered about it though and she tries to stay focused on having a good day.

November 24, 2010

Today is Katelyn's 18th birthday! We are calling this a celebration of her life because this summer we didn't know if she would still be alive to celebrate this birthday. The bad news first: At school today, two of Katelyn's favorite teachers came to one of her classes to sing "Happy

124

Birthday."

Most of the students in this class have turned into her enemies. These teachers try to get everyone to sing along with them, but only a few join in and the others just glare and roll their eyes. Katelyn said that she just sat there and smiled, but she wanted to cry. She is trying so hard to not let it bother her. Bless her heart. She has to take this every day. Later that day, one of those teachers came to get her out of class because she wanted to talk to her. As they stood in the hall, this teacher began to cry. She told Katelyn that she is so sorry, she had no idea that Katelyn is being treated this badly. She shared an experience with Katelyn about some things that happened to her when she was in high school. Katelyn needs to know that she is not the only one who has ever gone through something like this.

The good news: We didn't let the events of the day ruin the birthday. It turned out beautiful. It started at 1:00 and everyone was having so much fun, some didn't leave until 6:00.

"Is any one of you sick? He should call the elders of the church to pray over him and anoint him with oil in the name of the Lord. And the prayer offered in faith will make the sick person well..." James 5: 14-15 NIV

17. THOU ANOINTEST MY HEAD WITH OIL

No doubt one of the most recognized and memorized passages in the Bible is Psalm 23. I memorized this passage at an early age. And as a child going to Sunday School, I remembered the trick to getting the star by my name was to recite it as fast as I could so that the teacher would be impressed with my knowledge. I never really stopped to study or understand the meaning, but as an adult, I look to this scripture many times as guidance, and I understand it now, even the verse about anointing my head with oil.

In the New Testament of the Bible, Jesus called his disciples to him and gave them authority to drive out the evil spirits and to heal every disease and sickness. "They went out and preached that people should repent. They drove out many demons and anointed many sick people with oil and healed them." (Mark 6:12-13 NIV)

On an internet website, I typed in "what is the definition of anointing with oil" and these are the responses that I received. "Anointing with oil is the fastest way to send the demons screaming off into the night" and "anointing with oil is like turning on a signal flare to Heaven. It tells the Angels to give you special attention during this time." (21) I'm not sure if a Biblical scholar would agree with these definitions, but I do know through personal experience that God has given authority to Pastors and Elders of the church to anoint the sick people with oil and through prayer and faith, they will be healed.

In January 2011, six months into our journey with an eating disorder, we just started the second phase of the "re-feeding" process with Katelyn taking full control over her eating. During the next months, this freedom would be taken away and reinstated several times as she struggled with this emotional ordeal. When our children were babies, we fed them the nourishment that they needed in order to grow, and then we taught them how to feed themselves. We were reliving this in Katelyn's life, with her body getting stronger, but her mind still hearing the voices.

It was a chilly Sunday, and as with every other Sunday of our married life, we took our family to church. That's always been an important aspect of our roles as parents, that we take our children to church and to Sunday School to hear the Bible stories of Jesus. It makes me sad to think that future generations will not hear these Bible stories because so many parents don't take their children to Sunday School. I have been a Sunday School teacher for eighteen years, but I have to confess that when Katelyn became sick, I almost gave up that position. I confided in our Pastor that I couldn't teach the little children about God, when at that time, I didn't feel very close to God myself. He helped me to understand that is exactly how the devil wants us to feel. When trials and struggles enter our lives and we give up and turn away from God, then the devil wins. I will never let the devil win! I continued to teach my class and I continued to grow stronger in my faith through this experience.

On this Sunday morning, we had a special church service.

Our Pastor and Elders of the church asked for anyone who desired to be anointed with oil to come to the front of the church. As we sat in the pew, Trent glanced at me and I was half expecting him to roll his eyes as if to say "that doesn't really work." Earlier in the summer, we had a counseling session with our Pastor concerning Katelyn's illness and the Pastor wanted to anoint her with oil. Trent said no, he didn't believe in that. I was wrong today when I saw the look of pure compassion in his eyes as he grabbed Katelyn's hand and whispered to me, "You can stay here if you want to, but we are going to the front." No way was I staying behind, I was right behind them. The congregation was hushed in a reverent silence and the only sound was our soft sobs. I looked over my shoulder and saw my brother-in-law carrying his six year old son, who had been suffering from seizures for several months. The seizures had gotten so severe that he was having trouble walking, he fell a lot and he had missed a lot of school. Doctors ran many tests and prescribed medications, but no diagnosis had been made, and no medication stopped the seizures.

As our Pastor blessed Katelyn, my nephew and the others who had come forward, he anointed their heads with oil and said a prayer to God to please heal them of their diseases. We felt a sense of peace surround us as we wiped the tears from our eyes. We had walked that church aisle on complete faith, knowing fully in our hearts that God would heal our daughter and God would heal our nephew. As the scripture states, "the prayer offered in faith will make the sick person well." (James 5: 15 NIV)

Just a few weeks later, my nephew stopped having seizures altogether and Katelyn's recovery began a steady progress. We know that it wasn't the "oil" in the bottle that our Pastor used that helped them to heal. We know that it was the faith in our hearts. "Your faith has healed you." (Matthew 9:22 NIV.) "He saw that he had faith to be healed." (Acts 14:9 NIV.)

I truly believe that it wasn't a coincidence that God allowed our daughter and our nephew to experience life threatening illnesses at the exact same time and then bless them both with precious healing on the same day. I believe God planned this so that my sister-in-law and myself would create the special bond that we have today. As two mothers, who watched the suffering and pain of our children, we leaned on each other. We cried together through the trials and rejoiced together through the triumphs. We called and sent texts to each other daily; we sent each other cards, and we prayed for each other and for the healing of our children. Neither one of us would have made it through this without both of us holding on to each other and holding each other up.

As I write this chapter, it has been exactly one year since that special service. Katelyn has made a full recovery and my nephew has not had any more seizures. We just recently had another anointing of oil service at our church and many more people came forward this year. Some people even told Trent after the service that because they witnessed Katelyn's healing first hand, their faith has become stronger. Now they fully believe in the power of prayer, but, other people have told us they don't believe in "that stuff." Does that mean they don't believe in all parts of the Bible either?

January 23, 2011

We had a special service at church today. (I admit that I didn't even want to go to church today because sometimes I question God's plan.) Pastor asked anyone who needed healing to come to the front of the church to be anointed with oil. Trent was crying and he wanted to take Katelyn, so we all went before the church to have Katelyn anointed with oil and to ask for healing from this terrible disease. It was very emotional, but we all felt a sense of peace surrounding us. My brother-in-law took our nephew too.

Our prayer today is that Katelyn, our nephew and everyone else will be healed from their illnesses and that God will hear our prayers and answer our prayers.

"I thank God every time I remember you." Philippians 1: 3
NIV

18. BITTERSWEET

"The things that were the hardest for us to bear, became the things that were the sweetest for us to remember"
                                    - Lucius Annaeus Seneca

Katelyn has been an athlete all of her life. She started playing softball at an early age and hit her first "grand slam" when she was eight years old. She made the high school varsity softball team as a freshman and as a sophomore, she was named "Slugger of the Year" with the highest batting average on the team. She was also a member of the high school varsity cheerleading squad for three years.

Before school started in August 2010, Trent and I went to each coach at her high school to explain Katelyn's condition. We knew that the coaches, who had worked with her for so many years, would be shocked and concerned about her physical appearance. We met with the cheer coach, the softball coach, the "off season" coach, the athletic trainer and the athletic director. We needed their support, their understanding, their guidance and their professional input into helping us to do what was best for Katelyn's health. As a team, we would all work together to help her get well.

With the approval of our family doctor, the cheer coach was allowed to monitor Katelyn's cheerleading activities.

She could still be a part of the cheer team and this would help to regain her muscle strength, but her activities were limited. The softball coach and the "off season" coach monitored her weight. They took turns weighing her twice a week, charting her weight and texting me the information. They also provided healthy snacks for her during school because she needed to eat every few hours.

The athletic trainer monitored her during sports class. She wasn't allowed to do the running and weight lifting program until she gained some weight, so she sat in the bleachers every day and watched the other girls work-out. Another coach once told me that as Katelyn watched the other girls, she always encouraged them to do their best and to never give up.

The goal was for Katelyn to weigh one hundred pounds by January 2011 and then it would be decided if she could play softball in the spring. At one time, softball had been her life. Now, getting well was her life.

As the new year of 2011 approached, so did the decision about playing softball. Katelyn had regained fifteen pounds by now and was over the one hundred pound mark that our doctor and the coaches had set. It was hard to believe that just four months ago, she had weighed only eighty-five pounds. The coaching staff and our family were ecstatic about the weight gain, but we all had the same fear in the back of our minds. Would the stress of softball and the long hours of practice send Katelyn into a relapse? She had come so far with her recovery. None of us wanted to see her go backwards.

We discussed the decision with our doctor. He stated the exercise involved would be beneficial in getting her muscles strong and that she was at a healthy weight, but he was also concerned about the added stress. We discussed the decision with our dietician, who agreed fully with the doctor and finally, we discussed the decision with the softball coach who said that although it would be hard to replace Katelyn on the team, her health was more important.

Katelyn and I sat down and had a heart-to-heart talk. We knew that the only thing to do was to turn the decision of playing softball over to God. We wouldn't worry about it, we wouldn't think about it, we wouldn't talk about it; we knew that God would send an answer.

On January 24, 2011, with the help of God, Katelyn went by herself to tell the softball coach that she would not be playing softball. Although it was difficult, she felt a certain peace with the decision. The coach hugged her and they cried, and when the rest of the team heard the news, they all cried. Some said, "It just won't be the same without 'Kiesch' on first base." Others said, "Even though you won't be on the team, you will always be a part of the team."

I just couldn't bring myself to go watch the softball team play that year-this team that Katelyn had been a part of for so many years. But one day in March, I received a text message from Katelyn's sweet friend and teammate, Lyndsie. The text read "Please come to the softball game tonight at 6:00. It's important." Katelyn and Landee also received the same text message. As our family walked up to the softball field that day, my memories were bittersweet. I missed Katelyn playing softball, but I was so thankful that she was now healthy.

Then we saw the team warming up in their uniforms and we couldn't help but notice that each team member had a black band on their forearms. As we got closer, we could see that each player on the team was wearing a black band with "Kiesch # 4" embroidered in pink and as they gathered in a huddle before the start of the game, we heard them yell in unison, "This game is for Katelyn!" They wore those armbands at every game for the rest of the season. They even invited Katelyn to be a part of "Senior Night" before the last home game of the year.

What a special group of athletes who embraced Katelyn in her darkest hour and gave our family the sweetest memory. The 2011 VHS Softball team didn't win District that year, but all of those girls are winners in our eyes.

January 24, 2011

Katelyn decided not to play softball this year. She has really been struggling with this decision. She is worried about the stress and Trent and I said that we would support her no matter what her decision. She cried all week-end trying to make up her mind. She doesn't want the team to be disappointed in her, to think that she is a quitter. I told her that her true friends will support her and that if she is that unhappy, then maybe God is telling her that she shouldn't play. She made the decision on her own and she went to tell the coaches on her own and I am very proud of her. I will miss watching her play, but with everything she has been through emotionally and physically this year, I know that

134

her health is more important than anything.

April 19, 2011

The VHS softball team had "Senior Night" tonight and they asked Katelyn to be a part of it. She felt honored that they included her. Trent and I escorted her onto the field with the other seniors and their parents. Then all the seniors gave their mothers a rose. They all wrote a brief description of themselves and the announcer read it over the loudspeaker. Katelyn's was very emotional. In her speech, she told the other seniors and the rest of the team "Thank You" for being so supportive of her during her illness and she ended it with "A friend loves at all times." (Proverbs 17:17.) I don't think there was a dry eye on the field. Even the parents were crying. Landee said that she cried too! This illness has taught us so much about "friendship."

"For if you forgive men when they sin against you, your heavenly Father will also forgive you. But if you do not forgive men their sins, your Father will not forgive your sins." Matthew 6:14-15 NIV

19. FORGIVENESS

Forgive-such an easy word to say, such a hard thing to do. Ever since we were little kids, we have been told by parents, teachers, friends "You have to forgive and forget," or "kiss and make up," "turn the other cheek," "bury the hatchet." Sounds easy, doesn't it? If it were that easy, then there would never be broken marriages, broken families or broken friendships.

God wants us to forgive people who have hurt us. He never promised that it would be easy, but He did promise "Never will I leave you; never will I forsake you." (Hebrews 13:5 NIV) God wants us to ask Him in prayer for the guidance and the strength to forgive and then to pray for the people who have hurt us. In the "Lord's Prayer," Jesus tells us the way we should pray "Forgive us our debts, as we also have forgiven our debtors." (Matthew 6:12 NIV)

I know from personal experience that not forgiving is like poison flowing through your body. Every muscle in your body aches; your head aches; you can't sleep; you become bitter; you become depressed. You become imprisoned in something that only you can control. Corrie Ten Boom, a Christian woman who survived a Nazi concentration camp during the Holocaust said, "Forgiveness is to set a prisoner free, and to realize the prisoner was you."(22) Her parents and sister were murdered by the Nazi soldiers and yet she was able to forgive.

During our "journey through the valley", our family was deeply hurt by the actions and words of friends and even some family members. The description "deeply hurt" can't even begin to describe the gash in our hearts felt from the betrayal and mistrust; the sting felt from the rumors and lies; the destruction to our lives from the accusations and persecution. With the urging of the devil, our human instinct tells us to "get mad and then get even."

I'll be the first to admit that I listened to the devil's urging. I didn't want to forgive! I had been hurt; my children had been hurt! I wanted to stay mad! I wanted to wallow in hatred and self-pity! I reasoned with myself that these people didn't deserve forgiveness! But I knew deep down that I was wrong, and I knew that I was only hurting myself by not forgiving, and I knew that this was not what Jesus would do or would want me to do. Still, I just couldn't bring myself to do what needed to be done, to forgive.

One night, on one of the many nights I couldn't sleep, I decided that instead of just tossing and turning in bed, I would get up and do something productive. So, I put on my tennis shoes at 3:00 A.M. and went into the other room to walk on the treadmill. As I was walking, I began to pray, and as I was praying, I began to talk to God out loud. I walked and talked and prayed and cried as I desperately poured out my heart to God because of the pain and suffering that I was feeling. I was carrying on such a loud conversation with God that Trent heard me through the air vents. I wasn't angry with God; I just wanted God to feel my pain. I just knew that He couldn't possibly understand what I was feeling, so I stretched my arms out to my side to show God how much I was hurting and in a split second, I saw a glimpse of Jesus hanging on the cross with his arms stretched out. He was bleeding. He had been beaten and tortured, and then I realized the pain and the suffering, the humiliation and the rejection, the rumors and the lies, the accusations and the persecution that Jesus had gone through. It all made sense now. God had a plan and God included my family in the very small "fellowship" of people who have actually felt some of what Jesus felt…lies, persecution, rejection, hurt, and friends turning away. Jesus did this for my sins, for the sins of the world. And as He hung there on the cross, His words were not of hate or anger. His words were not "they don't deserve to be forgiven." His words were, "Father, forgive them, for they do not know what they are doing." (Luke 23:34 NIV)

November 30, 2010

> *We had our family devotion tonight on "forgiveness." We try to tell our kids that we need to forgive the people who have hurt us. Wow, is that hard! It's hard to forgive someone who has hurt you deeply. It's even harder to forgive someone who has hurt your children deeply. My prayer is that God will teach us about forgiveness and show us how to forgive as Jesus forgave. Katelyn said that it is so hard every day going to school and have people ignore her or roll their eyes at her, but she says she just smiles and tries to be nice. She says she wants*

them to see that she is being like Jesus and that Jesus is shining through her life.

May 9, 2011

My prayer all year long has been that God would change the hearts of the people that have been so mean to Katelyn this year. Sometimes we lose patience and we want God to act now. We have a hard time waiting on the Lord. We forget that God is in control and God has a plan.

Today, that prayer was answered. The one girl who has been the meanest to Katelyn, texted her and asked for forgiveness for being so mean. This person said that watching Katelyn this year go through everything that she went through and remain positive and remain a Christian has taught them many things. Katelyn told this person that she forgives them and that she will pray for them.

"Take my yoke upon you and learn from me, for I am gentle and humble in heart and you will find rest for your souls." Matthew 11:29 NIV

20. LEARNING TO DANCE IN THE RAIN

We truly believe that God allowed our family to go through this trial for a reason, but God didn't put us through this test to just sit back and observe. He wants us to learn and grow in our faith and then to share our experience with the world. Always remember, "You have to go through a test before you have a testimony." (23)

Sometimes God allows painful things to happen in our lives to wake us up and move us in a different direction. Sometimes we get so comfortable in our lives that we don't see that God has something else planned for us. Trent uses an illustration of cattle. A herd of cattle are very content in a grassy pasture, but the rancher needs to move them in a different direction. If they won't move, he uses a "hot shot" to get them to move. So the next time something painful happens in your life, instead of asking God "why," ask God, "what do you want me to learn from this?" and "what direction do You want me to go?" (24)

February 23, 2011

Lessons I have learned through this journey.

1. FULLY RELY ON GOD- He has a plan. He is in control. He knows all and He sees all. He will see us through this. Katelyn reminded me that the

acronym F.R.O.G. helps us to remember to *Fully Rely On God.*

2. *PATIENCE*- God's plan isn't complete until He says it's complete. Be patient and still and wait on the Lord to reveal His full plan.

3. *COMPASSION*- Everyone is going through some kind of trial in their life. Care about people. Don't get too involved in your own life to miss the opportunity to reach out to a friend in need. Call someone, send a card, pray for them and let them know you care about them and you are there for them. Teach this to your children and your grandchildren, so that you can make a difference in someone's life.

4. *FORGIVENESS*- Oh, how hard it is to forgive people who have hurt you. How even harder it is to forgive people who have hurt your children. How hard it is to forgive family members whom you trusted. God knows the pain and He sees the hurt and He wants to see how we handle it. Do we get bitter and spiteful and seek revenge or do we forgive and pray for our enemies and for those who hurt us? Remember, God knows firsthand what it feels like to watch His only Son be hurt, rejected and persecuted. He knows our pain too!

5. *WALK DAILY WITH THE LORD, NOT JUST ON SUNDAYS*- Just like with earthly fathers, we can't

ignore them all week, never talk to them, never acknowledge them, never speak to them and then on Sundays, when we need something, like money, we finally go to them. How would our earthly fathers feel? Well, our Heavenly Father is just like that. He doesn't want us to just come to Him only when we need something. He wants us to talk to Him during good times and bad times. Talk to Him daily. Walk with Him daily. Share your hurts, your worries, your burdens, and your joy. Talk to God just like you would talk to a friend. He is your friend.

6. BE A TESTIMONY OF FAITH- Sometimes it's not the trials that you are going through that gets other people's attention. It's how you act during these trials. People are watching you. Show them that God is at work in your life even during trials.

7. BE LESS JUDGMENTAL- No one knows what a person is going through unless you have actually "walked a mile in their shoes." Don't be so judgmental of someone just because they are different from you. Who gives any of us the right to "cast the first stone?" (John 8:7 NIV) No one is without sin and since we were all created equally in God's own image, then we are all equal. Instead of judging someone or "looking down your nose" at someone, reach out to them and give them a helping hand. The last thing a person needs if they are

142

going through a difficult time in their life is criticism, gossip, rumors and judgmental comments. They need prayers, love and support!

8. PRAY-PRAY-PRAY!!!- Don't just save your prayers for nighttime when you tuck your kids into bed. Pray continuously, all day, every day. Pray while you're driving, while you're walking, while you're in the shower, before you eat, before you go to bed, before you get out of bed in the morning, in the middle of the night, at ball games, at meetings, while you work, while you play. And our prayers should not be meek as if we are afraid to bother God. He already knows our wants, our needs, our hurts, even before we do. Cry out to God with a fervent heart. Show God that you are passionate and sincere. He is listening!

9. PRAISE GOD DURING THE STORM- It is so easy to praise God and to thank God when everything is going good in our lives, but what about during the difficult times in our lives? God is with us during the good and the bad times, so if we thank God for the good things, why not also thank Him for the bad things? This is easier said than done, but God assures us that He will never leave us nor forsake us, no matter what we are going through. Praise God during the sunshine and during the storm.

"And we, who with unveiled faces all reflect the Lord's glory, are being transformed into His likeness with ever-increasing glory, which comes from the Lord, who is the Spirit." 2 Corinthians 3:18 NIV

21. IN THE MIDST OF FIRE--GOD IS THERE

One day a women's Bible study group wondered what this Bible verse meant, "He will sit as a refiner and purifier of silver." (Malachi 3:3 NIV) They wanted to know what this verse was saying about God. One of the women in the group offered to do some research on the process of refining silver. She called a silversmith and made an appointment to watch him work.

While he worked, he explained that in the process of refining silver, one has to hold the silver in the midst of the fire where the flames are the hottest to burn away all the impurities. The woman asked the silversmith if it was true that he had to sit there in front of the fire the whole time. The man answered yes, that not only did he have to sit there holding the silver, but he also had to keep his eyes on the silver the entire time it was in the fire. If the silver was left a moment too long in the flames, it would be destroyed. "How do you know when the silver is fully refined?" she asked. He smiled at her and said, "Oh that's easy. When I see my image in it."

If today, you are feeling the heat of the fire, remember that God has His eye on you and will keep watching you until He sees His image in you! And whatever you are going through, you will be a better person in the end! (25)

Also remember, after the storms of life have passed, look

at the puddles of water left around your feet. Now look into those pools of water and see God's reflection looking back at you.

REFLECTIONS

November 25, 2010 Thanksgiving Day

We have so much to be thankful for today! Tanner is home from college and doing well. Katelyn had a wonderful birthday and is doing well with her eating. Landee had a wonderful basketball game on Tuesday and is doing good in school. Trent's jobs are increasing and money is finally starting to come in again. I have a beautiful family who are all healthy!
Thank You, God!

December 12, 2010

Today was the St. Paul School Christmas program. Katelyn is a Teacher's Aide, so she helped with the program. Landee and I went to watch our nephew who was in the program, and we sat in the balcony of the church. As the congregation sang "Silent Night" with all the lights off and everyone holding burning candles, I looked down at Katelyn sitting in the front row with all the little children and tears filled my eyes as I thought about how far we have come since this summer.

I thought about how we almost lost her. I thought about the people who have been so supportive--the high school counselor who allowed Katelyn to have a free period after lunch so she could have a longer lunch break and not be rushed . I thought about the high school science teacher who allowed Katelyn to do all her work online so that she would have a free period in the morning to have longer to eat breakfast. I thought about the high school secretaries who allowed Katelyn to come into their offices, shut the door and cry when she was having a bad day at school. I thought about the love of her supportive friends.

December 24, 2010 Christmas Eve

Today was Christmas Eve and it was such a good day. Katelyn was the Director of our church's children's Christmas program. She wrote the program, organized it and directed it. She is so good with kids and everyone complimented her work on the program. I'm proud of her for volunteering for this. She said that she wanted to give something back to God for all He has done to heal her.

When we got home, we had our family devotion and it was calm and peaceful, just like we imagined it was over two thousand years ago on that very first Christmas. After we all went to bed, Trent and I talked for over two hours as we remembered the past few months that we have been through. I

146

couldn't sleep at all and for once it wasn't because of worry or fear. I was actually at peace and so thankful for the life that God has given to us and the protection that He has provided for us.

I am so thankful for Katelyn and the progress that she is making and for the things she has taught me. I am so thankful that she is home for Christmas because if certain people would have had their way, she would be in a rehab right now and not be home for Christmas with the family who loves her.

I am so thankful that God gave us the insight that we needed to be her rehab at home, and that He let her stay home with us. I am so thankful for Trent; he is patient and understanding about my depression and that he is closer to God than ever before in his life. There is nothing more powerful than a praying husband and father!

January 1, 2011 New Year's Day

Today, I reflect back on the past year...I think about this summer in New Orleans with our church youth group. I was so worried about Katelyn and her eating and the heat and all the walking we did. I prayed so much that week. I bought Katelyn and myself matching bracelets that said "Believe," and we vowed that we would each wear our bracelet until the day that she was better. We have stopped wearing those bracelets now, but we still "believe."

I think about the true friends that reached out to us with phone calls, texts, cards and what a blessing it is to have them and I think about the "friends" we used to think were close friends and how they never once called to ask how we were doing. I feel like they turned their backs on us. It amazes me how times of trial bring out the best and worst in people.

I think about how the motto in our house has become "Be the Better Person" and how hard that is sometimes. I think this has taught our kids something. Like the other day, I overheard Landee saying that when she was sick and missed school, her friend never called to check on her, but when that same friend was sick, Landee said, "I will be the better person and call her to see how she feels."

I think what we have been through has made us more compassionate toward other people who are hurting. I have noticed that the people who have reached out to us, have also gone through trials in their lives, but the people who haven't reached out to us, have not gone through trials, YET!

I think it is sad that it takes something like this to make us be the "Better Person" but I thank God that He sent us these trials to help us to grow!

January 2, 2011

Trent hugged Katelyn today and said "My daughter is back!" I so desperately want to believe that and I firmly believe that God is working miracles in her life.

"Always be prepared to give an answer to everyone who asks you to give the reason for the hope that you have." 1 Peter 3:15 NIV

22. THE REASON FOR HOPE

In April, 2011, Katelyn, Landee and I went to see the newly released movie "Soul Surfer" about a thirteen year old girl from Hawaii, Bethany Hamilton, who had her arm bitten off by a shark while she was surfing. Even after going through this tragedy and losing an arm, she was determined to not only surf again, but also to compete in surfing competitions. Through this movie, she was able to tell the story of her faith and to become a witness for God.

At the end of the movie, Bethany was asked by a reporter if she could go back in time to the day of the shark attack, would she choose not to go surfing that day. Bethany replied, "If I hadn't gone surfing that day, then I wouldn't have been given the chance to embrace more people with one arm then I ever could with two arms." (26)

I think she was saying that if the accident had never happened, then she would never have become a witness for God. We also know that if we had never gone through Katelyn's illness, then our family would never have become witnesses for God.

The reason for this book is to share with you the wonderful power and grace of God. The reason for our hope came to us through the many friends, who shared inspirational Bible verses, devotions and God inspired ideas. All of these helped us during this time and hopefully they will help other families in difficult situations.

Fighting the devil by yourself is a losing battle. Fighting the devil with the full armor of God will prove to be victorious. "Put on the full armor of God so that you can take your stand against the devil's schemes. Stand firm then with the belt of truth; the breastplate of righteousness; shoes of readiness; shield of faith; helmet of salvation and the sword of the spirit, which is the word of God." (Ephesians 6: 11-17 NIV)

We began our fight against the devil by focusing on the word of God. We started by having nightly family devotions. This is something that we used to do regularly when our kids were little, but as they got older, we became too busy and used this as an excuse to push God to the bottom of the list. These nightly devotions became our top priority whether we were busy or not. We even had our devotions in the car traveling home from late night ball games.

One of the devotions that really touched us, especially with having two teenage daughters, who tend to look for worldly beauty instead of inner beauty, was by a famous actress who many people admired.

The Beauty Secrets of Audrey Hepburn

"For attractive lips--Speak words of kindness"
"For lovely eyes--Seek out the good in people"
"For a slim figure--Share your food with the hungry"
"For beautiful hair--Let a child run his fingers through it daily"
"For poise--Walk with the knowledge you'll never walk alone."

"That's good advice. Ask God to give you the Master Makeover from the inside out. Ask Him to develop the fruits of the spirit in your life: love, joy, peace, longsuffering, kindness, goodness, faithfulness, gentleness and self-control. (Galatians 5:22 NIV) If you do, you'll become a beautiful creature on the inside, which is sure to spill over onto your outer appearance." (27)

Another inspirational idea was given to me by a close friend who is a counselor and works at the State Hospital. She suggested that we keep mother/daughter journals. So I went to the local dollar store and bought two colorful journals, one for Katelyn and one for Landee. Every day, I would write a short message in each journal and place the journals on the girl's desks in their rooms. The message could be about anything, maybe something funny that had happened that day or something encouraging that I heard on the radio. Sometimes the message was serious and sometimes silly, but in each message, I wanted both girls to know how much I love them, I am proud of them, and that together we would make it through this. The girls would then write a message back to me and put the journals somewhere in my bedroom. When Katelyn left for college, we stopped writing in our journals, but looking back at some of the messages that were written, I know that we will always cherish these journals.

Another idea suggested by a friend was to put Bible verses on index cards and place these in the girls' rooms. Each week, I put the index cards with new verses in their rooms where I knew they were sure to see them. My hope was that every week, as they read the Bible verse over and over again, they would begin to memorize it. There is nothing more powerful than being in a difficult situation and being able to recall a special Bible verse that you have memorized. What started out as a way to encourage my daughters, turned into a big encouragement for me. Each week, as I studied the Bible looking for just the right verse, I gained so much knowledge and I began to memorize them too. I carry these index cards full of God's word in my purse now and it's reassuring to know that at any given time, I can reach in, select a card and be uplifted at that moment. I encourage you to memorize your favorite Bible verses or write them down on index cards and always have one ready so that you can text, send in a card, or share with a friend going through difficult times.

Entries from our Mother/Daughter Journals

September 13, 2010

Katelyn, I am so proud of the progress that you are making with your thoughts about food. You are eating so good, but I am really worried that you are

not gaining weight! I know that gaining weight is scary for you but you have to be mature about this and know that your body is not at a healthy weight right now! Read your Bible verse this week-I DID NOT make this up! "After all, no one ever hated his own body, but he feeds and cares for it, just as Christ does the church." Ephesians 5:29 NIV
You have to feed and care for your body!
Love Mom

September 13, 2010

Mom, It's so hard to express the scary thoughts that run through my mind about gaining weight, trying new foods, and adding calories, etc... I need ALL the support from you, Dad, Landee and Tanner that I can get. Please. I still cannot see me as being "unhealthy" because I feel like I am in such good shape and it is so hard to grasp and understand why people say I am an "unhealthy weight." I am still very confused about many things but I know I need help and I am asking for you and daddy to PLEASE continue helping and supporting me 100%! I love you so much!
Katelyn

December 22, 2010

*Dear Mom, I haven't written in this in a long time,
but I guess my life is going good, but I don't know
why I feel depressed and I wish I didn't worry about
stuff so much. I've been praying to stop worrying,
but it doesn't help. I love you so much Mom. Thanks
for being there for me.*

Love Landee

December 22, 2010

*Landee, I will pray for you that you aren't
depressed. We all go through a time of sadness and
depression. You have been through a lot these past
few months, going to high school, new teachers,
harder classes and making new friends. And then
watching your sister as she is trying to recover from
this illness and hearing people talk about her at
school. Then getting mad and wanting to fight
people because you want to take up for her. Then
the CPS case and being scared about that and
trying to forgive.*

*So you have every right to get sad and depressed
sometimes, but it's what you do with those feeling
that matters! Grandma went through a time of
depression and when I was growing up, she used to
tell me "You have to fight depression." You cannot
let depression control your life! So when I get sad
and depressed, I fight it by thinking about all the
good things in my life and not focusing on the*

154

negative things!!! When you feel like you are getting depressed, just say to yourself, "I am not going to be depressed because..." and start naming all the good things in your life that you have to be happy about! Let me know how that works because if you don't start feeling better, we can go to the doctor for some medicine or we can go to a counselor so you can talk to someone! I love you very much and I am always here for you!

Love, Mom

"Therefore, if anyone is in Christ, he is a new creation; the old has gone, the new has come." 2 Corinthians 5:17 NIV

EPILOGUE

As a little girl, I remember going to Vacation Bible School every summer and singing this song, "I've got the joy, joy, joy down in my heart." One of the verses that I tried to sing as fast as I could went like this, "I've got the peace that passes understanding down in my heart." Now try to sing that three times as fast as you can, and my little girl ears only heard, "I've got the peas that passes under Stanley down in my heart." I had no clue as a child or even as an adult what "peace that passes understanding" meant, until God sent our family on this journey. Through this trial, along with any other trials that our family may face, we have learned to turn everything completely over to God, who will, in turn grant us peace. A peace so powerful that we cannot explain it or understand it. A peace so powerful that other people will question how we can remain so calm during such adversity. A peace so powerful that we can rest assured that no matter the outcome, God is in full control.

As I began to write the ending to our journey, we all know that as long as the devil roams the earth, we will have our share of problems and trials, and we will never live happily ever after on this earth.

So, our family philosophy became: If the devil is so threatened by the Christian witness in our lives that he has to constantly throw his pitchfork at us, then we say "Bring it on!" "Because as for me and my household, we will serve

156

the Lord!" (Joshua 24:15 NIV) And all praise be to the Lord, because of His wonderful grace, we WILL live happily ever after in that beautiful place He has prepared for us in Heaven!

Our hope and help comes from God, who not only walked with us through the valley, but sometimes carried us in His arms when we didn't have the strength to take one more step. Our story does have a happy ending. Katelyn did make a full recovery, but it's sad to think that many people, who hear the devil's whisper in their ear, will not experience a happy ending. They will not experience a full recovery.

For a whole year, Katelyn lived the nightmare of this mental illness, known as Anorexia. She was tormented day and night by this illness, but she never took her eyes off of God, and she never lost her faith in Him. She was determined to persevere more than ever and to let Jesus shine through her life.

God saw her obedience. He healed her body and her mind, and He blessed her in immeasurable ways. She was voted "Most Loveable" by her senior class. She was nominated to be a member of the Valentine's Day Court. She was voted "All School Favorite" by the entire student body of her school. She was named the academic third ranking student of her class and received numerous scholarships to help pay for college.

At the high school that she attended, the tradition is that the Valedictorian and the Salutatorian give a speech, but the third ranking student has the opportunity to say a prayer at graduation. Katelyn said that it was a honor to be able to say a prayer in front of the hundreds of people who attended the graduation and to be a witness for God because of the miracles in her life.

After high school graduation, one of the most bittersweet experiences a parent will ever face is when a child leaves home for college. Undoubtedly, the most difficult experience that I have ever faced in my life was letting Katelyn go to college after the year that we had just been through. However, she was ready, she was healthy, and we knew she wasn't alone. Not only did Tanner attend the same college, but we know that God is there too! Katelyn is doing well at college; she has made a 4.0 for every semester, and has made some wonderful lifelong friends while continuing to be an everyday witness of God.

As for the rest of our family, we are grateful that God gave us this learning experience. Our son Tanner has graduated from college and has learned to turn his decisions over to God. Landee is doing well in school, she is active in our church's youth group, and she strives to be a Christian influence on other kids in her school. I am devoting my time to educating people about Eating Disorders, and Trent, well, let's just say that he has become a new creation in Christ. Recently, he had the wonderful opportunity to travel to Kenya, in Africa, on a two week mission trip to provide eye glasses to the native people and share the gospel of Jesus Christ. A year ago, he never would have considered going on such a trip. He would have many excuses why he couldn't go on such a trip, such as, he was too busy or he couldn't be away from his job for that long, or he wouldn't know what to say to people who asked him to share his faith. Today, he wants to shout from the mountain tops about the wonderful glory and grace of our amazing God. From Anorexia to Africa, what an incredible journey God has allowed our family to travel through.

"But those who hope in the Lord will renew their strength. They will soar on wings like eagles; they will run and not grow weary; they will walk and not be faint." Isaiah 40:31 NIV.

Twelve Things People Don't Understand About An Eating Disorder (28)

1. Eating Disorders aren't just about body image: Many people who struggle with Anorexia/Bulimia also present psychiatric conditions such as depression, anxiety disorders, obsessive compulsive disorder (OCD) which often develop into dangerous coping mechanisms.

2. Eating Disorders aren't just adolescent disorders: In a 2012 study from the Internal Journal of Eating Disorders-13% of women surveyed, who had an Eating Disorder, were over 50.

3. Eating Disorders aren't just women's disorders: In a 2011 study published in BMJ, 10-15% effected by Eating Disorders are male, but men are less likely to seek treatment.

4. Eating Disorders aren't just "white" disorders: Studies show that more African American girls suffer from Eating Disorders than previously recorded.

5. Eating Disorders aren't punch lines: Joking about Eating Disorders allow misconceptions that Eating Disorders aren't serious, that they are a conscience choice, that only vain girls live with them.

6. Eating Disorders are life consuming:
These anxieties have a way of swallowing up time, whether it is in hours lost to thoughts dominated by food or years lost in waiting for a goal, a size, a weight that will never be reached.

7. Eating Disorders are more than Anorexia, Bulimia, Binge-eating:
They include compulsive exercising, fixating on specific foods, or combined characteristics of multiple disorders.

8. People with Eating Disorders aren't easy to identify. You don't have to be underweight:
Symptoms include:
   A. Muscle Loss
   B. Electrolyte imbalance
   C. Irregular heartbeats
   D. Osteoporosis
   E. Ulcers
   F. High or low blood pressure
   G. Diabetes

9. People with Eating Disorders can't just "snap out of it":
Recovery isn't a matter of simply choosing to eat healthy. The most effective treatment programs include therapy, nutrition counseling, support groups, psychiatric medication, support from family and friends.

10. People with Eating Disorders don't see themselves the way you see them. This is called "Body Dysmorphic Disorder" or BDD: People with BDD perceive an exaggerated or imagined physical flaw in themselves.

11. Eating Disorders are serious and life threatening problems:
They have the highest mortality rate of any mental disorder and up to 24 Million people of all ages have an Eating Disorder in just the U.S.

12. Recovery is possible with the proper treatment:
What recovery looks like will vary from case by case, but for many it can include maintaining a healthy weight, restoring positive body image and living a full and long life.

VALUABLE TOOLS FOR FAMILIES
DEALING WITH EATING DISORDERS (29)

BE PATIENT: It is important to remember that just as it takes a long time for someone to develop an eating disorder, it may take a long time to recover from one as well. There is no quick fix or cure. Because changes in thinking and behavior happen slowly, the road to recovery takes time. Try to look at eating behaviors and weight gain weekly rather than daily.

EAT TOGETHER: Meals and snack times are often the most difficult part of the day for people with eating disorders. They may be anxious at meal times and feel guilty for eating. Meal times will require support and supervision. If someone they trust eats with them, the experience can be more comfortable.

KEEP CONVERSATION POSITIVE: Discuss neutral topics rather than focusing on food, calories, or weight. Try to talk about something fun, like your favorite sport teams, hobbies or music.

ADOPT A MEALTIME AGREEMENT: Agree in advance not to discuss eating thoughts such as portion size, calories, carbohydrate, or fat content at meal times. People with eating disorders have continuous negative thoughts about food. Mealtime agreements often work to reduce tension and stress associated with eating.

PLAN AHEAD: As a family, agree on the structure of

mealtimes: what time you will eat, the content of the meal, and who will be present at the meal.

GROCERY SHOP TOGETHER: If the person recovering from an eating disorder is ready for this, explore your favorite grocery store or visit a different market. Check out new foods and set a goal to try one new food each week. During recovery, it is important to increase food choices. A nutritionist can be helpful with setting goals and coaching a patient.

MAKE SURE THAT ALL FOODS YOU NEED FOR MEALS ARE AVAILABLE: This helps lessen worry at mealtime. Sometimes, if a food item is not available at the designated eating time, it can lead to panic and restricted food intake.

COOK TOGETHER AND TRY NEW RECIPES: Many patients with eating disorders like to cook with someone they trust. Learning how to cook provides another skill towards recovery. Trying new recipes also helps increase the "safe foods" list.

ENCOURAGE NEW INTERESTS: Suggest new activities such as art classes, volunteering, community service, and clubs at school, music or yoga. It is important to replace the unhealthy, disordered eating behaviors (excessive exercising or restrictive eating) with healthy interest. People struggling with eating disorders often choose activities that are based on dieting, weight regulation, and exercise. It is difficult to break away from these patterns. However, developing new interests can help reverse the disordered eating behaviors and over time improve self-esteem.

PLAN A SPECIAL EVENT: Make an appointment for a new haircut, manicure or massage. While recovering from an eating disorder, body shape, facial structure, hair texture, and overall appearance may change. They often feel they do not deserve special things. A special event can be a nice way of helping adjust to a new look. It also sends the message that they deserve to treat themselves to something special.

SHOP FOR CLOTHES: Because clothing sizes often fluctuate during recovery, it's best to buy a few new pieces of clothing at a time rather than an entire wardrobe. Some eating disorder patients have a difficult time clothes shopping because of dressing room mirrors. It can also be difficult for them to buy a different size than they are used to. Ask first if they would like to go shopping or if they would prefer that you pick up new items for them.

AVOID COMMENTING DIRECTLY ON PHYSICAL APPEARANCE OR BODY SHAPE:
Statements or questions such as "You look great!" or "You look better", "You've gained weight" or "You've lost weight-what's going on?" often makes them feel extremely uncomfortable. During recovery, they often look much healthier, brighter, and stronger. However, commenting on this is often interpreted negatively. A remark such as "You

look so much better now that you're not all skin and bones" may be interpreted as "I am fat!" by a person with an eating disorder.

COMMENT ON HEALTH AND ENERGY LEVEL: Statements such as "You are full of energy" or "You look well rested" are more appropriate and often make them feel supported in their recovery. These types of conversations show recognition of health status and do not focus on body shape or size.

SMILE! HAPPINESS IS CONTAGIOUS: A bright, cheerful and consistently positive attitude works wonders. It is very difficult to watch someone you care about struggle with any illness. Worried looks or tears often make them feel guilty about their eating disorder and may lead them to feel more anxiety, self-loathing, and depression. It is very important to try to be positive. A simple smile can spread a message of hope and cheer. Sharing positive thoughts about body image is also very helpful.

REFERENCES

1. Webster's New World College Dictionary, Fourth Edition. Copyright 2002 by Wiley Publishing, Inc., Cleveland, Ohio.

2. Stone, Faith. *A Mother's Intuition*. The Baby Corner.com.

3. Maudsley Parents.org.

4. Brown, Harriet. *Brave Girl Eating-A Family's Struggle with Anorexia*. New York, New York: William Morrow, 2010.

5. American Psychiatric Association. *Practice Guidelines for the Treatment of Patients with Eating Disorders*. 2nd Ed., Washington, D.C., 2000:6-7.

6. Brown, Harriet. *Brave Girl Eating-A Family's Struggle with Anorexia*. New York, New York: William Morrow, 2010.

7. Brown, Harriet. *Brave Girl Eating-A Family's Struggle with Anorexia*. New York, New York: William Morrow, 2010.

8. Author Unknown. *Anorexia Facts*. Health Status.com.

9. Author Unknown. *Anorexia Facts*. Health Status.com.

10. Wentz, Izabella. *Hashimoto's Thyroiditis: Lifestyle Interventions for Finding and Treating the Root Cause.* Lexington, Kentucky. 2015.

11. 91.5 FM Radio KCBI Dallas/Fort Worth, TX. KSYE Frederick/Lawton, OK.

12. Wellman, Jack. *Does The Bible Say What The Devil Looks Like?* What Christians Want To Know.com.

13. Mayo Clinic Staff. *Broken Heart: Can Grief Damage Your Heart?* Mayo Clinic.com.

14. DiMarco, Hayley. *Mean Girls.* Grand Rapids, Michigan: Revell a division of Baker Publishing Group, 2008.

15. Meltzer, Bernard.

16. Goodman, Don. Hobbs, Becky. *Angels Among Us.* RCA Records. *1993.* Alabama Country/Western Band.

17. Kroll, Woodrow. *God Loves You Even When You Are Dethroned.* Back To The Bible. 91.5 FM Radio KCBI Dallas/Fort Worth, TX.

18. Texas Legislative Council. *Texas Family Code.* 1963.

19. Niebuhr, Reinhold. *The Serenity Prayer.*

20. Courtic, K. *Bringing Elizabeth Home.* Dateline NBC.

21. Mueller, Errol. *The Mystical Rites of Our Creator.* *H*ome Worship 101.com.

22. Fairchild, Mary. *Forgiveness.* Christianity About.com Guide.

23. Vanzant, Lyanla. The Oprah Winfrey Show. Harpo Productions.

24. Warren, Rick. *The Purpose Driven Life.* Grand Rapids, Michigan: Zondervan, 2002.

25. Author Unknown. *In The Midst of Fire-God is There.*

26. Hamilton, Bethany. *Soul Surfer (film).* 2011, Directed by Sean McNamara.

27. Daily Grace for Teens-Devotional Reflections to Nourish Your Soul. *Extreme Makeover.* Colorado Springs, Colorado: Honor Books, 2005.

28. BuzzFeed.com/Arianna Rebolini & Helen Nigatu BuzzFeed Staff.

29. Center for Young Women's Health at Boston Children's Hospital.

* Scripture is taken from the Holy Bible, New International Version NIV. Grand Rapids, Michigan: Zondervan, 1986.

* Scripture is taken from the Holy Bible, King James Version KJV, Family Record Edition. Wichita, Kansas: Devore & Sons, 1985.

* Scripture is taken from the Message Bible, MSG. Colorado Springs, Colorado: NavPress, 2002.

Back Cover: Top photo, The Kieschnick Family on family vacation 2014.

Bottom photo, recent picture of Katelyn Kieschnick celebrating her healthy recovery.

Made in the USA
San Bernardino, CA
12 September 2015